WATKINS

CLASSIC RECIPES™

pil

Publications International, Ltd.

Favorite Brand Name Recipes at www.fbr

Microwave Cooking: Microwave ovens vary in wattage. Use the cooking times as
guidelines and check for doneness before adding more time.

Table of Contents

Brunch Delights

Wake up to the tantalizing aroma of cinnamon rolls, muffins or coffeecake. These tasty breads and other breakfast treats are the perfect way to start your day off right.

Poppy Seed Bread

BREAD

   3 cups all-purpose flour

$1^1/_2$ teaspoons salt

$1^1/_2$ teaspoons WATKINS Baking Powder

$2^1/_4$ cups granulated sugar

   3 eggs

$1^1/_2$ cups milk

   1 cup plus 2 tablespoons WATKINS Original Grapeseed Oil

$1^1/_2$ to 4 tablespoons WATKINS Poppy Seed

$1^1/_2$ teaspoons WATKINS Vanilla

$1^1/_2$ teaspoon WATKINS Almond Extract

$1^1/_2$ teaspoons WATKINS Butter Extract

GLAZE

   $^3/_4$ cup powdered sugar

   $^1/_4$ cup orange juice

   $^1/_2$ teaspoon WATKINS Vanilla

   $^1/_2$ teaspoon WATKINS Almond Extract

   $^1/_2$ teaspoon WATKINS Butter Extract

Preheat oven to 350°F. Grease and flour two $8^1/_2 \times 4^1/_2$-inch loaf pans. Combine all bread ingredients in large bowl in order listed above; beat 2 minutes. Pour into prepared pans. Bake for 55 minutes or until toothpick inserted into centers comes out clean.

Meanwhile, blend all glaze ingredients in small bowl until smooth. Drizzle over bread while loaves are warm. *Makes 2 loaves*

Favorite recipe from **Susan Residence, Minnesota**

Pfannkuchen (German Pancake)

4 eggs

1 cup skim milk

$^1/_2$ cup all-purpose flour

2 tablespoons sugar

$2^1/_2$ teaspoons WATKINS Vanilla

$^1/_2$ teaspoon salt

$1^1/_2$ tablespoons butter

Apple Rhubarb Compote (recipe follows)

Preheat oven to 425°F. Combine eggs, milk, flour, sugar, vanilla and salt in large bowl; beat with wire whisk or rotary beater until smooth. Place butter in 10-inch ovenproof skillet; melt in oven just until butter begins to sizzle. Remove pan from oven; tilt to coat bottom with butter. Immediately pour batter into hot pan. Bake for 14 to 18 minutes or until pancake is puffed and golden brown.

Meanwhile, prepare Apple Rhubarb Compote. Fill pancake with compote immediately after removing pancake from oven. Cut into wedges. Serve immediately. *Makes 4 servings*

Apple Rhubarb Compote

2 cups peeled apple slices
$1/2$ cup thinly sliced rhubarb
2 teaspoons butter
$1/4$ cup apple cider or juice
$1/2$ teaspoon WATKINS Apple Bake Seasoning

Cook apples and rhubarb in butter in medium skillet over medium heat, stirring frequently, just until softened. Add apple cider and apple bake seasoning; simmer until apples are tender but still hold shape. Serve warm.

Breakfast Salad

1 apple, diced (with peel)
1 banana, sliced
$1/2$ cup sunflower seeds
$1/2$ cup raisins
$1/4$ cup chopped dates
2 tablespoons honey
1 tablespoon orange juice
1 teaspoon WATKINS Vanilla
$1/2$ teaspoon WATKINS Ground Cinnamon
1 cup cottage cheese
4 melon halves

Combine apple, banana, sunflower seeds, raisins, dates, honey, orange juice, vanilla and cinnamon in medium bowl; toss to blend. Spoon cottage cheese evenly into melon halves; top with fruit mixture.

Makes 4 servings

9

Homemade Granola

2 cups uncooked old-fashioned oats

1 cup flaked coconut

$^1/_2$ cup sunflower seeds

$^1/_4$ cup ($^1/_2$ stick) butter

$^1/_4$ cup brown sugar

$^1/_4$ cup honey

1 $^1/_2$ teaspoons WATKINS Vanilla

1 teaspoon WATKINS Ground Cinnamon

$^1/_4$ teaspoon WATKINS Nutmeg

$^1/_2$ cup toasted wheat germ

1 cup raisins

$^1/_2$ cup dried fruit bits (apricots, raisins, apples)

Preheat oven to 300°F. Combine oats, coconut and sunflower seeds on large baking sheet with sides; mix well and spread out evenly. Bake for 20 minutes, stirring several times. Meanwhile, combine butter, brown sugar, honey, vanilla, cinnamon and nutmeg in small saucepan. Cook, stirring constantly, over medium heat until butter is melted and mixture is well blended. Remove from heat.

Remove baking sheet from oven; increase oven temperature to 350°F. Add wheat germ to oat mixture on baking sheet. Pour warm honey mixture over oat mixture; stir with spoon or spatula until thoroughly coated. Return to oven and bake for 5 minutes. Stir in raisins and dried fruit bits; mix well and spread out evenly. Return pan to oven and bake for 5 to 10 minutes or until golden brown. Pour granola onto large piece of foil; cool completely. Store in airtight container for up to 2 weeks.

Makes 6 cups (12 servings)

Cream Cheese Coffeecake

1^1/$_4$ cups (2^1/$_2$ sticks) butter, softened, divided
1^3/$_4$ cups granulated sugar, divided
   2 eggs
2^1/$_2$ cups all-purpose flour, divided
   2 teaspoons WATKINS Baking Powder
 ^{1}/$_2$ teaspoon salt
3^1/$_4$ teaspoons WATKINS Vanilla, divided
   2 packages (8 ounces each) cream cheese, softened
   1 egg yolk
   1 teaspoon WATKINS Ground Cinnamon
 ^{1}/$_2$ cup powdered sugar
   1 tablespoon milk

Preheat oven to 350°F. Grease 13×9-inch baking dish. For batter, beat 1 cup butter and 1 cup granulated sugar in large bowl until blended; add eggs and beat well. Combine 2 cups flour, baking powder and salt. Gradually add flour mixture to butter mixture until blended. Stir in 2 teaspoons vanilla.

For filling, beat cream cheese, ^{1}/$_2$ cup granulated sugar, egg yolk and 1 teaspoon vanilla in medium bowl until smooth. For topping, combine remaining ^{1}/$_2$ cup flour, ^{1}/$_4$ cup granulated sugar, ^{1}/$_4$ cup butter and cinnamon; mix with fork until crumbly.

Spread half of batter into prepared baking dish; spread cream cheese filling over batter and spoon remaining batter on top. Smooth surface with knife or spatula. Sprinkle with topping. Bake for 40 to 45 minutes or until toothpick inserted into center comes out clean. Cool in pan on wire rack. Blend powdered sugar, milk and remaining ^{1}/$_4$ teaspoon vanilla in small bowl until smooth. Drizzle over coffeecake. Refrigerate leftovers.

Makes 15 servings

Oven French Toast

Butter
3 eggs, well beaten
3/4 cup milk
1 tablespoon sugar
1 1/2 teaspoons WATKINS Clear Vanilla Extract
1/8 teaspoon WATKINS Nutmeg
8 slices day-old French or white bread
1/2 teaspoon WATKINS Ground Cinnamon mixed with
2 tablespoons sugar (optional)
Pancake syrup (optional)

Preheat oven to 500°F. Generously grease 15×10×1-inch pan with butter. Beat eggs, milk, sugar, vanilla and nutmeg in shallow bowl until well blended. Heat pan in oven for 1 minute; remove from oven. Dip bread slices, one at a time, into egg mixture. Arrange on hot pan. Drizzle any remaining egg mixture over bread.

Bake for 7 to 10 minutes or until bottoms of bread slices are golden brown. Turn bread, bake for 3 to 5 minutes longer or until golden brown. Sprinkle with cinnamon-sugar mixture or serve with syrup, if desired.

Makes 4 servings

Tip: To make ahead, dip and arrange bread in greased, unheated pan; cover with plastic wrap and refrigerate for 2 to 3 hours or overnight. Bake as directed above.

Fresh Apple Bundt Cake

2¹/2 cups all-purpose flour

1 tablespoon WATKINS Baking Powder

¹/2 teaspoon WATKINS Nutmeg

¹/4 teaspoon baking soda

1 cup sugar

¹/2 cup (1 stick) butter, softened

¹/4 cup buttermilk

2 teaspoons WATKINS Vanilla

¹/2 teaspoon WATKINS Lemon Extract

1 cup egg substitute, thawed if frozen

2 medium Golden Delicious apples, peeled, cored and diced
    (about 2 cups)

Powdered sugar for garnish

Preheat oven to 350°F. Spray 10-inch bundt or tube pan with WATKINS Cooking Spray; dust with flour and tap out excess. Combine flour, baking powder, nutmeg and baking soda in medium bowl. Combine sugar, butter, buttermilk and extracts in large bowl; beat with electric mixer about 4 minutes until pale and creamy. Alternately add flour mixture and egg substitute; beat until well blended and fluffy. Stir in apples with spoon or spatula. Spread batter into prepared pan.

Bake for 50 to 60 minutes or until golden brown and toothpick inserted near center comes out clean. Cool in pan on wire rack 10 minutes; turn out of pan and cool completely on wire rack. Dust with powdered sugar.

Makes 12 servings

Dazzling Orange Quick Bread

BREAD

    1 cup all-purpose flour

    1 cup whole wheat flour

    3/4 cup packed light brown sugar

    1/4 cup WATKINS Vanilla Dessert Mix

    1 teaspoon baking soda

    1 teaspoon WATKINS Baking Powder

    1 teaspoon WATKINS Ground Cinnamon

    1 teaspoon WATKINS Nutmeg

    1/2 teaspoon salt

    2/3 cup diet orange soda

    1/2 cup honey

    3 tablespoons egg substitute

    1 teaspoon WATKINS Butter Extract

    1/2 cup ground pecans

    1 can (11 ounces) mandarin oranges, drained and chopped

GLAZE

    1 cup powdered sugar, sifted

    1 to 2 tablespoons hot milk

    1 teaspoon WATKINS Vanilla

    1/2 teaspoon WATKINS Orange Extract

    1/2 cup honey-roasted pecan halves or coarsely chopped pecans

Preheat oven to 350°F. Grease and flour 9×5-inch loaf pan. For bread, combine flours, brown sugar, dessert mix, baking soda, baking powder, cinnamon, nutmeg and salt in large bowl. Add orange soda, honey, egg substitute and butter extract; mix well. Stir in ground pecans and mandarin oranges. Pour into prepared pan. Bake for 50 to 60 minutes or until toothpick inserted into center comes out clean. Cool in pan on wire rack for 10 minutes; remove from pan and cool completely on wire rack.

For glaze, combine powdered sugar, milk and extracts in small bowl; beat until smooth. Drizzle over cake in lattice fashion. Arrange pecan halves between lattices or sprinkle with chopped pecans.   *Makes 12 servings*

Favorite recipe from **Janice Green, Tennessee**

Dazzling Orange Quick Bread

Raspberry and Cream Cheese Coffeecake

$2^1/_2$ cups all-purpose flour

$^3/_4$ cup sugar, divided

$^1/_2$ cup (1 stick) butter

1 cup sour cream

4 egg whites, divided

2 teaspoons WATKINS Vanilla, divided

1 teaspoon WATKINS Almond Extract

$^1/_2$ teaspoon WATKINS Baking Powder

$^1/_2$ teaspoon baking soda

$^1/_4$ teaspoon salt

1 package (8 ounces) cream cheese

$^1/_2$ cup all-fruit raspberry preserves

$^1/_4$ cup sliced almonds

$^1/_2$ teaspoon WATKINS Ground Cinnamon

Preheat oven to 350°F. Spray 9- or 10-inch springform pan with WATKINS Cooking Spray and coat lightly with flour. Combine flour and $^1/_2$ cup sugar in large bowl; cut in butter with pastry blender or two forks until mixture resembles coarse crumbs. Reserve 1 cup crumbs for topping. Add sour cream, 2 egg whites, $1^1/_2$ teaspoons vanilla, almond extract, baking powder, baking soda and salt to remaining crumb mixture; mix well. Spread batter over bottom and 2 inches up side of prepared pan. (Batter should be about $^1/_4$ inch thick on side.)

Combine cream cheese, remaining ¼ cup sugar, 2 egg whites and ½ teaspoon vanilla in small bowl; mix well. Pour over batter in pan. Carefully spoon raspberry preserves over top. Combine reserved crumb mixture, almonds and cinnamon; sprinkle evenly over preserves.

Bake for 40 to 50 minutes or until crust is golden brown. Cool 15 minutes on wire rack. Remove side of pan; serve warm or cool completely. Refrigerate any leftovers.   *Makes 12 servings*

Cheese Blintzes

12 Vanilla Crêpes (page 20)

2 packages (8 ounces each) cream cheese, softened

1 cup cottage cheese

1 egg

3 tablespoons powdered sugar

1 teaspoon WATKINS Vanilla

1/2 teaspoon WATKINS Almond Extract

1/2 can (21 ounces) blueberry pie filling (reserve remainder
     for another use)

1/2 cup sour cream

2 tablespoons granulated sugar

1/2 teaspoon WATKINS Clear Vanilla Extract

1 tablespoon butter

Prepare Vanilla Crêpes. Combine cream cheese, cottage cheese, egg, powdered sugar and extracts in medium bowl with electric mixer at medium speed until smooth. Place 1/4 cup cheese filling in center of browned side of each crêpe; fold left and right sides over filling and overlap ends to enclose filling.

Heat blueberry pie filling in small saucepan over low heat; keep warm. Combine sour cream, granulated sugar and clear vanilla in small bowl; mix well.

Melt butter in large skillet over medium heat. Cook half of filled blintzes at a time until golden. Serve hot with warm blueberry pie filling and sour cream topping.

Makes 12 servings

continued on page 20

Cheese Blintzes

Cheese Blintzes, continued

Vanilla Crêpes

1 1/2 cups milk
3 eggs
2/3 cup all-purpose flour
2 tablespoons melted butter, plus additional butter for skillet
1 teaspoon WATKINS Vanilla
1/2 teaspoon salt
1/8 teaspoon WATKINS Ground Cinnamon

At least 2 hours before making crêpes, blend milk, eggs, flour, 2 tablespoons butter, vanilla, salt and cinnamon in medium bowl with wire whisk. Refrigerate for 2 hours. Brush 7-inch crêpe pan (or any rounded nonstick skillet) lightly with additional melted butter; heat over medium heat until drop of water sizzles and rolls off surface of skillet.

Pour in scant 1/4 cup batter, tilting to coat bottom of skillet. Cook 1 minute or until top of crêpe is set. Loosen edges with rubber spatula, shaking pan gently to loosen. Invert onto waxed paper. Repeat with remaining batter; stacking crêpes between layers of waxed paper. Use crêpes for Cheese Blintzes, Crêpes Suzette or other recipes requiring crêpes. *Makes 12 crêpes*

Vanilla Butter

1/2 cup (1 stick) butter, softened
1/4 cup powdered sugar
1 teaspoon WATKINS Vanilla

Combine butter, sugar and vanilla in small bowl; beat until smooth. Use as spread for sweet breads or muffins. *Makes 1/2 cup*

Peach Coffeecake

$^1/_2$ cup (1 stick) butter, softened

$^3/_4$ cup plus 2 tablespoons sugar, divided

1 egg, at room temperature

1$^1/_2$ cups all-purpose flour

1$^1/_2$ teaspoons WATKINS Baking Powder

$^1/_2$ cup plain yogurt or sour cream

2 teaspoons WATKINS Vanilla

$^1/_2$ teaspoon WATKINS Peach Extract

1 cup chopped fresh, frozen or canned peaches, well drained

$^3/_4$ cup chopped pecans

$^1/_2$ teaspoon WATKINS Nutmeg

Preheat oven to 400°F. Grease 8-inch square baking dish. Beat butter in large bowl until smooth. Add $^3/_4$ cup sugar; beat until mixture is light and fluffy. Add egg; beat until well blended. Combine flour and baking powder in small bowl. Beat yogurt and extracts into butter mixture; stir in flour mixture. Add peaches and pecans, stirring just to blend. Spoon batter into prepared baking dish.

Combine remaining 2 tablespoons sugar and nutmeg; sprinkle over batter. Bake for 28 to 30 minutes or until lightly browned and toothpick inserted into center comes out clean.   *Makes 12 servings*

Homemade Cinnamon Rolls

$4^{1}/_{4}$ to $4^{3}/_{4}$ cups all-purpose flour, divided

1 package quick-rising active dry yeast

$1^{1}/_{4}$ cups plus 4 to 5 teaspoons milk, divided

$^{1}/_{4}$ cup granulated sugar

$^{1}/_{4}$ cup ($^{1}/_{2}$ stick) plus 6 tablespoons butter, softened, divided

2 teaspoons WATKINS Vanilla, divided

5 teaspoons WATKINS Ground Cinnamon, divided

1 teaspoon salt

2 eggs

$^{1}/_{2}$ cup packed brown sugar

1 cup powdered sugar

Combine $1^{1}/_{2}$ cups flour and yeast in large bowl. Heat $1^{1}/_{4}$ cups milk, granulated sugar, $^{1}/_{4}$ cup butter, 1 teaspoon vanilla, 1 teaspoon cinnamon and salt just until mixture is warm (120° to 130°F), stirring constantly. Add to flour mixture with eggs; beat with electric mixer at low speed for 30 seconds, scraping side of bowl often. Beat at high speed for 3 minutes.

Stir in as much remaining flour as possible with spoon (dough will be soft). Knead in enough remaining flour to form moderately soft dough, 3 to 5 minutes total. Shape dough into a ball; place in lightly greased bowl, turning once. Cover and let rise in warm place about 1 to $1^{1}/_{2}$ hours until double in size. (Dough is ready to shape when you can lightly press two fingers $^{1}/_{2}$ inch into dough and indentation remains.) Punch down dough and divide in half. Place each half on lightly floured surface and smooth into a ball. Cover and let rest 10 minutes.

Preheat oven to 350°F. Grease 13×9-inch baking pan. Roll half of dough into 12×8-inch rectangle on lightly floured surface. Spread with 3 tablespoons butter. Combine brown sugar and remaining 4 teaspoons cinnamon; sprinkle half of mixture over dough. Roll up dough from short side; seal edge by brushing with water. Repeat with remaining dough. Slice one roll into 8 pieces and other into 7 pieces. Arrange slices cut sides up in prepared pan. Cover; let rise about 30 minutes or until nearly doubled.

Bake for 25 to 40 minutes or until light brown. Immediately invert rolls onto wire rack, then invert again. Cool slightly on wire rack. Combine powdered sugar, remaining 4 teaspoons milk and 1 teaspoon vanilla in small bowl; drizzle glaze over rolls. Serve warm or store in airtight container. *Makes 15 rolls*

Homemade Cinnamon Rolls

Easy Apple Kuchen

1³/₄ cups sugar, divided
¹/₂ cup (1 stick) butter, softened
2 eggs
2¹/₂ teaspoons WATKINS Vanilla
1 teaspoon WATKINS Butter Extract
3 cups all-purpose flour
2 teaspoons WATKINS Baking Powder
³/₄ teaspoon salt
1 cup milk
5 cups peeled apple slices
1 teaspoon WATKINS Apple Bake Seasoning

Preheat oven to 375°F. Grease 13×9-inch baking dish. Beat 1¹/₂ cups sugar and butter in large bowl with electric mixer until light and fluffy. Blend in eggs and extracts. Combine flour, baking powder and salt in separate bowl; add to sugar mixture alternately with milk, mixing well after each addition. Pour into prepared baking dish; arrange apple slices on top.

Combine remaining ¹/₄ cup sugar and apple bake seasoning; sprinkle over apples. Bake for 35 to 40 minutes. Serve warm or cold.

Makes 15 servings

Vanilla Muffins

1 cup plus $1^{1}/_{2}$ teaspoons sugar, divided

1 egg, beaten

2 cups all-purpose flour

2 teaspoons WATKINS Baking Powder

$^{1}/_{8}$ teaspoon salt

1 cup milk

$^{1}/_{4}$ cup ($^{1}/_{2}$ stick) butter, melted

$2^{1}/_{2}$ teaspoons WATKINS Vanilla

$^{1}/_{8}$ teaspoon WATKINS Ground Cinnamon

Vanilla Butter (optional, page 20)

Preheat oven to 375°F. Grease 12 muffin pan cups. Combine 1 cup sugar and egg in large bowl; beat with electric mixer at medium speed until well blended. Combine flour, baking powder and salt; add to sugar mixture alternately with milk, beginning and ending with flour mixture and beating well after each addition. Stir in butter and vanilla.

Spoon batter into prepared pan, filling muffin cups two-thirds full. Combine remaining $1^{1}/_{2}$ teaspoons sugar and cinnamon; sprinkle evenly over muffins. Bake for 15 to 20 minutes. Remove muffins from pan immediately. Serve warm with Vanilla Butter, if desired.

Makes 12 muffins

French Toast

2 eggs, lightly beaten
$^1/_2$ cup milk
$^1/_2$ teaspoon WATKINS Vanilla
$^1/_4$ teaspoon salt
6 slices day-old bread
1 tablespoon butter

Combine eggs, milk, vanilla and salt in shallow bowl; mix well. Dip bread slices in egg mixture. Melt butter in large skillet; cook bread until golden brown on both sides. Serve hot with maple syrup, powdered sugar or tart jelly.

Makes 3 servings

Creamy Fruit Dip

1 package (8 ounces) cream cheese, softened
1 container (8 ounces) vanilla yogurt
$^1/_2$ cup honey
1 teaspoon WATKINS Vanilla
$^1/_2$ teaspoon WATKINS Ground Cinnamon
$^1/_2$ teaspoon WATKINS Nutmeg

Beat cream cheese in medium bowl until smooth. Add yogurt, honey, vanilla, cinnamon and nutmeg; mix until blended. Cover and refrigerate at least 1 hour to blend flavors. Serve with fresh fruit dippers.

Makes 1$^1/_2$ cups

French Toast

Watkins Products are the kind of things that are in use in every home, every day. The things that mean repeat orders every trip.

Every Home is
A Prospect For

Watkins
Products—

Tea Cake with Rum Sauce

1 1/2 cups vanilla wafer crumbs

1 cup finely chopped pecans

1 1/2 cups (3 sticks) butter, softened, divided

2 1/3 cups sugar, divided

1/2 teaspoon WATKINS Ground Cinnamon

4 eggs

1 cup milk

2 teaspoons WATKINS Vanilla

2 2/3 cups all-purpose flour

1 1/2 teaspoons WATKINS Baking Powder

1/2 teaspoon salt

Rum Sauce (recipe follows)

Preheat oven to 350°F. Generously grease two 9×5-inch loaf pans. Combine vanilla wafer crumbs, pecans, 1/2 cup butter, 1/3 cup sugar and cinnamon in small bowl; press onto bottom and 1 inch up sides of prepared pans.

Beat remaining 2 cups sugar and 1 cup butter in large bowl until light and fluffy. Add eggs; mix well. Combine milk and vanilla in small bowl. Sift flour, baking powder and salt into medium bowl. Add milk mixture and flour mixture alternately to sugar mixture, beating well after each addition. Pour batter over crust in loaf pans.

Bake for 60 to 75 minutes. Turn cakes onto wire racks to cool. Serve with Rum Sauce.   *Makes 20 servings*

Rum Sauce

1 $^3/_4$ cups milk

$^1/_2$ cup sugar

$^1/_3$ cup WATKINS Vanilla Dessert Mix

$^1/_4$ cup ($^1/_2$ stick) butter

$^1/_2$ teaspoon WATKINS Rum Extract

Combine milk, sugar and dessert mix in medium saucepan; heat over medium heat until mixture comes to a boil. Stir in butter; heat until melted. Remove from heat and stir in rum extract. Serve warm. Sauce can be cooled and reheated before serving.   *Makes about 2$^1/_2$ cups*

Best-Loved Cakes

From the simple Apple Cake to the showstopping Lady Baltimore Cake, there's something here for every occasion. Cheesecakes, chocolate cakes, fruit-filled cakes and more will make unforgettable endings to any meal.

Carrot Cake with Black Walnut Frosting

1 cup granulated sugar

3 eggs

$^2/_3$ cup WATKINS Original Grapeseed Oil

1 teaspoon WATKINS Vanilla

$1^1/_2$ cups all-purpose flour

2 teaspoons WATKINS Ground Cinnamon

$1^1/_2$ teaspoons baking soda

1 teaspoon WATKINS Baking Powder

$^1/_2$ teaspoon WATKINS Ground Cloves

$^1/_2$ teaspoon WATKINS Nutmeg

$^1/_2$ teaspoon WATKINS Allspice

$^1/_2$ teaspoon salt

2 cups finely grated carrots

1 cup walnuts, chopped

1 package (8 ounces) cream cheese

$^1/_3$ cup butter, at room temperature

$^1/_2$ teaspoon WATKINS Vanilla Nut Extract

$^1/_2$ teaspoon WATKINS Black Walnut, Butter Pecan, Butter Nut or Vanilla Nut Extract

$2^1/_2$ cups powdered sugar

continued on page 32

Carrot Cake with Black Walnut Frosting, continued

Preheat oven to 350°F. Spray two 9×2-inch round cake pans with
WATKINS Cooking Spray; dust with flour. Combine granulated sugar,
eggs and oil in large bowl; beat for 1 minute. Stir in vanilla. Add flour,
spices, baking soda, baking powder and salt; beat about 1 minute. Fold
in carrots and walnuts. Pour into prepared pans. Bake for 30 minutes or
until toothpick inserted into center comes out clean. Beat cream cheese,
butter and extracts in medium bowl until smooth. Add powdered sugar,
$^1\!/_2$ cup at a time; beat until frosting is of spreading consistency. Fill and
frost cake with frosting.   *Makes 12 servings*

Variations: Add golden raisins or pineapple to batter, if desired. Or,
substitute 2 cups shredded zucchini for the shredded carrots.

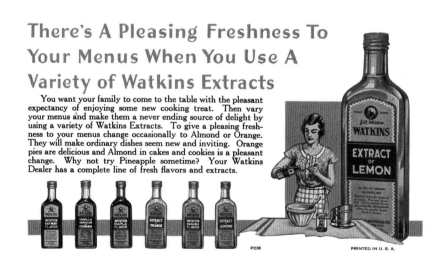

Marbled Pumpkin Cheesecake

$1^{1}/_{2}$ cups gingersnap cookie crumbs (about 32 cookies)

$^{1}/_{4}$ cup ($^{1}/_{2}$ stick) unsalted butter, melted

2 packages (8 ounces each) cream cheese, softened

$^{3}/_{4}$ cup sugar, divided

1 teaspoon WATKINS Vanilla

3 eggs

1 cup canned or cooked pumpkin

$1^{1}/_{2}$ teaspoons WATKINS Pumpkin Pie Spice

Preheat oven to 400°F. Combine cookie crumbs and butter; press firmly onto bottom and up side of 9-inch pie pan. Bake for 5 minutes; remove from oven and let cool. Reduce oven temperature to 325°F.

Beat cream cheese, $^{1}/_{2}$ cup sugar and vanilla in large bowl until blended. Beat in eggs, one at a time. Reserve 1 cup batter. Add remaining $^{1}/_{4}$ cup sugar, pumpkin and pumpkin pie spice to remaining batter; mix well. Alternately layer pumpkin and plain batters over partially baked crust. Cut through batters with knife several times for marbled effect.

Bake for 45 to 50 minutes or until cheesecake springs back when lightly touched. Loosen cheesecake from rim of pan. Let cool to room temperature, then chill. *Makes 12 servings*

Almond Meringue Torte

1 1/4 cups plus 2 teaspoons sugar, divided
1/2 cup vegetable shortening
4 large eggs, separated
5 tablespoons milk
2 teaspoons WATKINS Vanilla
1 cup sifted cake flour
1 teaspoon WATKINS Baking Powder
1/4 teaspoon plus pinch salt
      Pinch cream of tartar
1/2 cup sliced almonds, toasted
1/2 teaspoon WATKINS Ground Cinnamon
2 cups Vanilla Whipped Cream (page 35)
      Assorted fresh fruit for garnish

Preheat oven to 350°F. Grease two 9-inch round cake pans. Beat 1/2 cup sugar and shortening in medium bowl until light and fluffy. Add egg yolks, one at a time, beating well after each addition; stir in milk and vanilla. Combine flour, baking powder and 1/4 teaspoon salt; add to sugar mixture and beat until smooth. Pour into prepared pans. Beat egg whites with pinch salt and cream of tartar until soft peaks form. Add 3/4 cup sugar, 1 tablespoon at a time, until stiff, glossy peaks form.

Divide meringue between pans, spreading over batter and mounding slightly in center. Sprinkle with almonds and remaining 2 teaspoons sugar mixed with cinnamon. Bake for 25 to 30 minutes or until toothpick inserted into centers comes out clean. Cool in pans on wire racks 5 minutes; turn out onto racks to cool completely. (Use second rack to invert cake layers again so meringue is right side up.) Save any almonds that may fall off for garnish.

No more than 6 hours before serving, place one layer, meringue side up, on serving plate. Spread with ¾ cup Vanilla Whipped Cream. Top with remaining layer, meringue side up; pipe or spoon remaining Vanilla Whipped Cream around edge. Garnish with fresh fruit and any reserved almonds.
Makes 12 servings

Vanilla Whipped Cream (Crème Chantilly)

1 cup heavy whipping cream
2 to 4 tablespoons powdered sugar (depending on sweetness desired)
1 teaspoon WATKINS Vanilla

Chill small bowl and beaters of electric mixer in refrigerator (chill in freezer if in a hurry). Beat cream in chilled bowl until it begins to thicken. Add sugar and vanilla; beat until stiff. Do not overbeat.
Makes 2 cups

Tip: If you don't want to make real whipped cream, you can improve the flavor of the store-bought variety. Add 1 teaspoon Watkins Vanilla to 2 cups frozen, thawed whipped topping or when making packaged whipped topping.

Lady Baltimore Cake

White Cake Supreme (recipe follows)
Seven Minute Frosting (recipe follows), divided
$1/2$ cup chopped pecans
$1/3$ cup raisins, chopped
$1/3$ cup figs, chopped
$1/4$ cup chopped candied cherries (optional)
Additional candied cherries and chopped pecans for garnish (optional)

Prepare White Cake Supreme and Seven Minute Frosting. Combine $3/4$ cup frosting, pecans, raisins, figs and cherries, if desired, in medium bowl; mix well. Spread between cake layers. Frost top and side of cake with remaining frosting. Decorate top of cake with additional candied cherries and chopped pecans, if desired.   *Makes 12 servings*

White Cake Supreme

$2 1/4$ cups sifted cake flour
$1 1/2$ cups sugar
1 cup milk
$1/2$ cup vegetable shortening
$3 1/2$ teaspoons WATKINS Baking Powder
2 teaspoons WATKINS Vanilla or Clear Vanilla Extract
1 teaspoon salt
4 egg whites

Preheat oven to 350°F. Grease and flour two 9-inch round cake pans.
Combine flour, sugar, milk, shortening, baking powder, vanilla and salt in
large bowl; beat with electric mixer at low speed for 30 seconds, scraping
side of bowl occasionally. Beat at high speed for 2 minutes, scraping side
of bowl occasionally. Add egg whites; beat at high speed for 2 minutes.
Pour batter into prepared pans. Bake for 25 to 30 minutes or until
toothpick inserted into center comes out clean. Cool in pans on wire
racks 10 minutes; remove from pans and cool completely on wire racks.

Makes two 9-inch layers or one 13×9-inch cake (12 servings)

Seven Minute Frosting

1 1/2 **cups sugar**
1/2 **cup water**
2 **egg whites, unbeaten**
1 **tablespoon light corn syrup**
Dash salt
2 1/2 **teaspoons WATKINS Vanilla or Clear Vanilla Extract**

Combine sugar, water, egg whites, corn syrup and salt in top of double
boiler. (Do not place over water.) Beat about 1 minute with hand-held
electric mixer until well blended. Set pan over boiling water, making
sure bottom of pan does not touch water. Cook, beating constantly,
about 7 minutes or until frosting forms soft peaks. Remove pan from
boiling water. Add vanilla; beat until stiff peaks form.

Makes enough to frost tops and sides of two 8- or 9-inch cake layers

Cran-Raspberry Cake

    1 package light pound cake mix
1 1/2 teaspoons WATKINS Butter Extract
1 1/2 teaspoons WATKINS Vanilla
    1 pie filling recipe WATKINS Vanilla Dessert Mix
    1 cup cranberry or cran-raspberry juice cocktail
    2 cups fresh raspberries *or* 2 packages (10 to 12 ounces each)
        frozen raspberries, thawed
    2 tablespoons sugar
    8 ounces reduced-fat whipped topping
    Additional fresh raspberries for garnish

Prepare pound cake according to package directions, stirring extracts into batter. Bake according to package directions and cool completely. Prepare dessert mix according to package directions using recipe for pie filling; cool completely.

Cut pound cake into 1/2- to 3/4-inch slices; place one slice on each dessert plate. Drizzle each slice with 1 tablespoon juice, top with raspberries and sprinkle with 1/2 teaspoon sugar. Gently stir 1 cup whipped topping into pie filling and spoon mixture over raspberries. Top with remaining whipped topping. Refrigerate until ready to serve. Garnish with additional berries just before serving.   *Makes 12 servings*

Variation: For red, white and blue cake, add blueberries to the raspberries in the recipe.

Cran-Raspberry Cake

Scrumptious Vanilla Cheesecake with Caramel Topping

1 1/2 cups graham cracker crumbs

6 tablespoons unsalted butter, melted

1/4 cup packed brown sugar

1/2 teaspoon WATKINS Ground Cinnamon

4 packages (8 ounces each) cream cheese, softened

1 1/2 cups granulated sugar

5 eggs, at room temperature

1 tablespoon WATKINS Vanilla

2 teaspoons fresh lemon juice

Caramel Topping (recipe follows)

2 cups Vanilla Whipped Cream (page 35)

2 packages (1.4 ounces each) toffee candy bars, broken into pieces

Preheat oven to 350°F. Lightly butter 9-inch springform pan with 2 3/4-inch side. Combine graham cracker crumbs, butter, brown sugar and cinnamon in medium bowl; mix well. Press onto bottom and up side of prepared pan. Refrigerate crust while preparing filling.

Beat cream cheese in large bowl with electric mixer until fluffy. Gradually add granulated sugar and beat until smooth, scraping down side of bowl occasionally. Beat in eggs, one at a time. Beat in vanilla and lemon juice. Pour filling into chilled crust. Bake for about 1 hour and 15 minutes or until cake rises about 1/2 inch over rim of pan and center moves only slightly when shaken. Cool in pan on wire rack. (Cake will fall as it cools, sinking slightly in center.) Cover and refrigerate at least 6 hours until well chilled. Prepare Caramel Topping.

Cut around side of springform pan with sharp knife to loosen cheesecake; release pan side. Pour $^1/_3$ cup topping into center of cheesecake. (Refrigerate and save remaining topping as sauce for ice cream.) Chill cheesecake for about 2 hours or until topping is almost set. Just before serving, pipe Vanilla Whipped Cream decoratively around edge of cheesecake. Arrange toffee pieces in whipped cream border. Cut cake into small wedges. Refrigerate leftovers.   *Makes 16 servings*

Caramel Topping

    $^2/_3$ cup packed brown sugar

    $^1/_3$ cup light corn syrup

    2 tablespoons butter

    $^1/_8$ teaspoon salt

    $^1/_3$ cup heavy whipping cream or evaporated milk

    1 teaspoon WATKINS Caramel Extract

    $^1/_2$ teaspoon WATKINS Vanilla

Combine brown sugar, corn syrup, butter and salt in heavy medium saucepan. Cook over medium heat, stirring occasionally, until mixture comes to a boil and sugar is dissolved. Remove from heat and cool slightly, just until mixture begins to thicken. Slowly whisk in cream until blended. Stir in extracts; mix well. Let cool completely.

Bûche de Noël

¹/₃ cup all-purpose flour

¹/₄ cup WATKINS Pure Cocoa

1 teaspoon WATKINS Ground Cinnamon

³/₄ teaspoon WATKINS Ginger

¹/₄ teaspoon baking soda

Pinch WATKINS Cloves

Pinch freshly ground WATKINS Sea Salt

4 egg whites

¹/₂ cup granulated sugar, divided

2 egg yolks

3 tablespoons buttermilk

Powdered sugar

Coconut Filling (recipe follows)

Chocolate Frosting (page 44)

Marshmallow Mushrooms (page 44)

Preheat oven to 375°F. Coat 15×10-inch jelly-roll pan with WATKINS Cooking Spray. Line with waxed paper; spray waxed paper with cooking spray and dust with flour. Combine flour, cocoa, cinnamon, ginger, baking soda, cloves and salt in small bowl; set aside.

Beat egg whites in medium bowl with electric mixer until soft peaks form. Increase speed to high; gradually add ¹/₄ cup sugar, beating until sugar dissolves and stiff peaks form. Beat egg yolks and remaining ¹/₄ cup sugar in large bowl with same beaters until very thick and lemon colored; beat in buttermilk. Gently fold beaten egg whites into egg yolk mixture with rubber spatula or wire whisk, one third at a time. Gently fold flour mixture into egg mixture, one third at a time. Spread batter evenly in prepared pan. Bake 10 minutes or until top of cake springs back when lightly touched.

Sprinkle clean cloth or dish towel lightly with powdered sugar. Immediately invert hot cake onto towel. Peel off waxed paper and discard. Starting from long side, roll up cake with towel jelly-roll fashion. Cool cake completely, seam side down, on wire rack (about 1 hour).

To assemble, gently unroll cooled cake. Spread Coconut Filling over cake almost to edges with spatula. Starting from same long side, roll up cake without towel. Cut 1½-inch-thick diagonal slice from each end of roll with sharp knife; set aside. Place rolled cake, seam side down, on long platter. Spread some of Chocolate Frosting over roll but not on cut ends. Place one end piece on side of roll to resemble branch. Place remaining end piece on top of roll to resemble another branch. Spread remaining frosting over roll and branches, but not on cut ends. Make long strokes in frosting with tines of fork to resemble bark of tree. Refrigerate cake at least 2 hours before serving. Arrange Marshmallow Mushrooms around cake.   *Makes 10 servings*

Coconut Filling

    ⅓ cup evaporated milk
    ⅓ cup sugar
     1 egg, slightly beaten
     1 tablespoon butter
        Dash freshly ground WATKINS Sea Salt
    ⅓ cup flaked coconut
    ¼ cup chopped pecans
    ½ teaspoon WATKINS Vanilla

Combine milk, sugar, egg, butter and salt in small saucepan. Cook and stir over medium heat until mixture thickens and bubbles. Stir in coconut, pecans and vanilla. Cool completely.

continued on page 44

Bûche de Noël, continued

Chocolate Frosting

    3 tablespoons WATKINS Pure Cocoa
    1 tablespoons butter
    $^1/_2$ teaspoon WATKINS Vanilla
       Dash freshly ground WATKINS Sea Salt
    2 tablespoons very hot water
  1 $^1/_2$ cups powdered sugar

Combine cocoa, butter, vanilla and salt in medium bowl; mix well. Add hot water; stir until cocoa and butter are dissolved. Add powdered sugar; beat with electric mixer about 2 minutes. Add more powdered sugar or water as needed until frosting is of spreading consistency.

Marshmallow Mushrooms

    6 large marshmallows
    Chocolate Frosting
    WATKINS Pure Cocoa

Cut each marshmallow in half crosswise. Flatten half of each marshmallow for cap of mushroom. Roll other half between palms for stem. Attach caps to stems with frosting. Dust tops of mushrooms with cocoa.

Makes 6 mushrooms

Bûche de Noël

Guilt-Free Pound Cake

3 cups sugar

$^3/_4$ cup (1$^1/_2$ sticks) margarine, softened

1$^1/_2$ cups frozen egg substitute, thawed, *or* 8 egg whites

1$^1/_2$ cups nonfat plain yogurt or low-fat sour cream

1 teaspoon baking soda

4$^1/_2$ cups sifted cake flour

$^1/_2$ teaspoon salt

2 teaspoons WATKINS Vanilla

1 teaspoon WATKINS Butter Extract

Preheat oven to 325°F. Spray 10-inch bundt or tube pan with WATKINS Cooking Spray and coat lightly with flour. Beat sugar and margarine with electric mixer at medium speed until blended. Gradually add egg substitute (if using egg whites, add one at a time), beating until well blended. Combine yogurt and baking soda; mix well. Combine flour and salt. Add flour mixture and yogurt mixture alternately to sugar mixture, beginning and ending with flour mixture. Stir in extracts. Spoon batter into prepared pan.

Bake for 1 hour and 20 minutes or until toothpick inserted near center comes out clean. Cool in pan on wire rack for 10 minutes. Remove cake from pan and cool completely on wire rack.   *Makes 20 servings*

Lemon Pound Cake: Add 2 teaspoons Watkins Lemon Extract and decrease vanilla to 1 teaspoon.

Coconut Pound Cake: Add 1$^1/_2$ teaspoons Watkins Coconut Extract and decrease vanilla to 1 teaspoon.

Butter Rum Pound Cake: Add 1$^1/_2$ teaspoons Watkins Rum Extract and decrease vanilla to 1 teaspoon.

Pineapple Upside Down Cake

3 cans (8$^{1}/_{4}$ ounces each) sliced pineapple in juice

$^{1}/_{4}$ cup ($^{1}/_{2}$ stick) butter

$^{1}/_{3}$ cup packed light brown sugar

9 maraschino cherries

1 cup all-purpose flour

$^{3}/_{4}$ cup granulated sugar

1$^{1}/_{2}$ teaspoons WATKINS Baking Powder

$^{1}/_{4}$ teaspoon salt

$^{1}/_{4}$ teaspoon WATKINS Nutmeg

$^{1}/_{2}$ cup milk

$^{1}/_{4}$ cup vegetable shortening

2 teaspoons WATKINS Vanilla

1 egg

Vanilla Whipped Cream (page 35)

Preheat oven to 350°F. Drain pineapple, reserving 2 tablespoons juice. Melt butter in very heavy or iron ovenproof 10-inch skillet over medium heat. Add brown sugar, stirring until sugar is melted; remove from heat.

Arrange 8 pineapple slices over sugar mixture, overlapping slightly. Place one slice in center of pan; fill pineapple centers with cherries. Cut remaining slices into halves and arrange around edge of skillet. Combine flour, granulated sugar, baking powder, salt and nutmeg in large bowl. Add milk and shortening; beat with electric mixer at high speed for 2 minutes. Add vanilla, egg and reserved pineapple juice; beat for 2 minutes. Pour batter over pineapple in skillet, spreading carefully. Bake for 40 to 45 minutes or until toothpick inserted into center comes out clean. Cool in pan on wire rack 5 minutes. Loosen edge of cake. Cover with serving platter and invert cake onto platter; remove pan. Serve warm with Vanilla Whipped Cream. *Makes 8 servings*

Cranberry Cheesecake

2 cups vanilla wafer crumbs
6 tablespoons butter, melted
3 packages (8 ounces each) cream cheese, softened
2 cups sugar, divided
1 tablespoon WATKINS Clear Vanilla Extract
4 eggs
2 cups fresh or frozen cranberries
$^1/_2$ cup water
3 tablespoons WATKINS Vanilla Dessert Mix

Preheat oven to 350°F. For crust, combine vanilla wafer crumbs and butter; press onto bottom and up side of 9-inch springform pan. Bake for 10 minutes. Reduce oven temperature to 325°F.

For filling, beat cream cheese, $^3/_4$ cup sugar and vanilla with electric mixer at medium speed until well blended. Add eggs, one at a time, mixing well after each addition. Pour filling over crust. Bake for 1 hour and 5 minutes. Loosen cake from rim of pan; cool completely on wire rack before removing rim of pan. Refrigerate until completely chilled.

For glaze, combine cranberries, 1 cup sugar and water; bring to a boil, stirring frequently. Boil about 2 minutes. Combine remaining $^1/_4$ cup sugar and dessert mix; stir into cranberry mixture. Bring to a boil, stirring frequently. Cool to lukewarm, then chill glaze 1 to 2 hours before spreading over cheesecake. (Or, cooled glaze can be spooned on cheesecake after slicing.) *Makes 12 servings*

Vanilla Filled Fudge Crown

    1 package ($18\frac{1}{4}$ ounces) Swiss or milk chocolate cake mix

$1\frac{1}{2}$ teaspoons WATKINS Ground Cinnamon

    1 package (8 ounces) cream cheese, softened

    2 tablespoons butter, softened

$1\frac{1}{2}$ tablespoons WATKINS Vanilla Dessert Mix

    1 can (14 ounces) sweetened condensed milk (not evaporated milk)

    1 egg

    2 teaspoons WATKINS Vanilla

    Glaze (recipe follows)

Preheat oven to 350°F. Generously grease and flour 10-inch bundt or tube pan. Prepare cake mix as directed on package, adding cinnamon before mixing. Pour into prepared pan. Beat cream cheese, butter and dessert mix in medium bowl until fluffy. Gradually beat in condensed milk, egg and vanilla until smooth. Pour evenly over cake batter in pan.

Bake for 50 to 55 minutes or until toothpick inserted near center comes out clean. Cool in pan 10 minutes. Remove from pan and cool completely on wire rack. Drizzle Glaze over cake. *Makes 14 servings*

Glaze

    1 cup powdered sugar

$\frac{1}{4}$ cup WATKINS Chocolate Dessert Mix

    2 tablespoons WATKINS Original Grapeseed Oil

$\frac{1}{2}$ teaspoon WATKINS Vanilla

    2 to 4 tablespoons warm milk

Combine powdered sugar, dessert mix, oil and vanilla in small bowl; mix well. Add enough milk to achieve desired drizzling consistency.

Apple Cake

    3 cups all-purpose flour
    3 cups sugar, divided
    4 eggs
    1 cup vegetable oil
 $^1/_2$ cup orange juice
    3 teaspoons WATKINS Baking Powder
 2$^1/_2$ teaspoons WATKINS Vanilla
    1 teaspoon salt
    4 large apples, peeled and sliced
    2 to 3 teaspoons WATKINS Ground Cinnamon

Preheat oven to 350°F. Grease and flour 10-inch tube pan. Beat flour,
2 cups sugar, eggs, oil, orange juice, baking powder, vanilla and salt in
large bowl for 2 minutes. Pour half of batter into prepared pan. Toss
apples with remaining 1 cup sugar and cinnamon in medium bowl.
Arrange half of apple mixture in one to two layers over batter. Top
with remaining batter; arrange remaining apple mixture over batter.

Bake for about 1 hour or until toothpick inserted near center comes
out clean. Cool cake in pan on wire rack. Invert onto serving plate.
(Slide knife around edge of pan if necessary to loosen cake from pan.)

Makes 12 servings

Apple Cake

Italian Cream Cake

¹/₂ cup (1 stick) butter or margarine, softened

¹/₂ cup vegetable shortening

2 cups sugar

5 eggs, separated

1 teaspoon baking soda

1 cup buttermilk

2 cups all-purpose flour, sifted twice

1 cup flaked coconut

1 cup chopped nuts

1 teaspoon WATKINS Vanilla

1 teaspoon WATKINS Coconut Extract

Cream Cheese Frosting (recipe follows)

Preheat oven to 350°F. Grease and flour bottoms of three 9-inch round cake pans. Beat butter, shortening and sugar in large bowl until creamy. Add egg yolks, one at a time, beating well after each addition. Stir baking soda into buttermilk in small bowl until dissolved; add to butter mixture alternately with flour. Beat in coconut, nuts and extracts.

Beat egg whites in medium bowl until stiff peaks form. Fold egg whites into batter. Pour into prepared pans, using 2 cups batter for each pan. Bake for 25 minutes. Cool in pans on wire racks for 10 minutes; remove from pans and cool completely on wire racks. Spread Cream Cheese Frosting between layers and on top of cooled cake. Refrigerate until ready to serve.

Cream Cheese Frosting

    1 package (8 ounces) cream cheese, softened
$^1/_2$ cup (1 stick) butter, softened
    1 package (16 ounces) powdered sugar
    1 teaspoon WATKINS Almond Extract

Beat cream cheese and butter until smooth. Add powdered sugar and almond extract; beat until light and fluffy.

Spicy Pumpkin Roll

3 eggs

1 cup granulated sugar

²/₃ cup mashed cooked pumpkin or canned pumpkin

1 teaspoon WATKINS Vanilla

³/₄ cup all-purpose flour

2 teaspoons WATKINS Pumpkin Pie Spice

1 teaspoon WATKINS Baking Powder

¹/₄ teaspoon salt

1 cup chopped pecans

1 cup plus 3 to 4 tablespoons sifted powdered sugar, divided

1 package (8 ounces) cream cheese, softened

2 tablespoons butter or margarine, softened

¹/₂ teaspoon WATKINS Butter Pecan Extract

Sweetened whipped topping flavored with WATKINS Vanilla
for garnish

Whole or chopped pecans for garnish

Preheat oven to 375°F. Grease 15×10-inch jelly-roll pan; line with waxed paper. Grease and flour waxed paper. Beat eggs in large bowl with electric mixer at high speed until thick; gradually add granulated sugar and beat 5 minutes. Stir in pumpkin and vanilla. Combine flour, pumpkin pie spice, baking powder and salt; gradually stir into pumpkin mixture until well blended. Spread batter into prepared pan; sprinkle with pecans. Bake for 12 to 15 minutes or until toothpick inserted into center comes out clean.

Sift 3 to 4 tablespoons powdered sugar into 15×12-inch rectangle on clean cloth or dish towel. Loosen cake from pan; immediately invert hot cake onto towel. Carefully peel off waxed paper and discard. Starting from narrow side, roll up cake with towel jelly-roll fashion. Cool cake completely, seam side down, on wire rack.

Beat cream cheese and butter with electric mixer at high speed until fluffy. Gradually add remaining 1 cup powdered sugar and butter pecan extract; beat until well blended. Unroll cake; spread with cream cheese filling and carefully re-roll. Place cake on serving plate, seam side down. Garnish or frost with whipped topping and pecans. *Makes 10 servings*

Spicy Pumpkin Roll

White Fudge Cake

$^3/_4$ cup (4 ounces) coarsely chopped white chocolate

$^1/_2$ cup hot water

$2^1/_2$ cups all-purpose flour

$1^1/_4$ cups sugar

1 cup (2 sticks) butter, softened

1 cup buttermilk or sour milk

1 teaspoon baking soda

$^1/_2$ teaspoon WATKINS Baking Powder

$^1/_4$ teaspoon salt

3 eggs

1 teaspoon WATKINS Vanilla

$^1/_2$ teaspoon WATKINS Almond Extract

$^1/_2$ cup chopped almonds

White Fudge Frosting (recipe follows)

Preheat oven to 350°F. Grease and flour two 9-inch round cake pans. Melt white chocolate with hot water in small saucepan over low heat, stirring frequently; cool. Combine flour, sugar, butter, buttermilk, baking soda, baking powder and salt in large bowl; beat with electric mixer at low speed just until moistened. Beat for 1 minute at medium speed. Add eggs, melted white chocolate mixture and extracts; beat for 1 minute at medium speed. Stir in almonds. Pour batter into prepared pans.

Bake for 30 to 35 minutes or until toothpick inserted into centers comes out clean. Cool in pans on wire racks 15 minutes; loosen edges and carefully remove cake layers from pans. Cool completely on wire racks. Place one cake layer, bottom side up, on serving plate; spread with frosting. Top with second layer, top side up. Spread frosting on top and side of cake.

Makes 12 servings

White Fudge Frosting

3/4 cup (4 ounces) coarsely chopped white chocolate
2 tablespoons WATKINS Vanilla Dessert Mix
1 cup milk
1 cup (2 sticks) butter, softened
1 cup sugar
1 teaspoon WATKINS Vanilla

Combine white chocolate and dessert mix in medium saucepan; blend in milk. Cook over medium heat, stirring constantly, until very thick. Cool completely. Beat butter, sugar and vanilla in medium bowl with electric mixer about 3 minutes or until light and fluffy. Gradually add cooled white chocolate mixture; beat at high speed until mixture reaches consistency of whipped cream.

Watkins Supreme Products are Family Favorites

Fabulous Pies & Tarts

Just thinking about a Brownie Pie à la Mode or Peaches and Cream Pie can make your mouth water. Homemade pies are guaranteed crowd-pleasers—year-round comfort food that no one can resist!

Harvest Time Praline Apple and Cranberry Pie

1$^1/_2$ cups packed brown sugar, divided

$^1/_2$ cup WATKINS Vanilla Dessert Mix

1$^1/_2$ teaspoon WATKINS Ground Cinnamon

6 cups peeled and sliced tart green apples

1$^3/_4$ cups fresh cranberries

2 tablespoons lemon juice

1 unbaked 9-inch pie crust

$^1/_2$ cup (1 stick) unsalted butter

2 tablespoons evaporated milk

1$^1/_2$ teaspoon WATKINS Vanilla

$^1/_2$ teaspoon WATKINS Caramel Extract

1 cup chopped walnuts

Preheat oven to 350°F. Combine $^3/_4$ cup brown sugar, dessert mix and cinnamon in large bowl. Add apples, cranberries and lemon juice; toss to coat. Spoon mixture into pie crust, mounding in center. Bake for about 1$^1/_2$ hours or until apples are tender. (Cover with foil during last 30 to 45 minutes to prevent overbrowning.) Transfer to wire rack; uncover and cool.

Melt butter with remaining $^3/_4$ cup brown sugar and milk in heavy skillet over low heat, stirring frequently. Increase heat to medium-high and bring to a simmer, stirring constantly. Remove from heat; stir in extracts, then walnuts. Pour mixture into medium bowl; let stand about 10 minutes or until slightly thickened and cooled, stirring occasionally. Spoon topping over pie, covering completely. Let stand about 30 minutes or until topping sets.

Makes 10 servings

Fresh Fruit Tart

Pastry for single-crust 10-inch pie
1 package (8 ounces) reduced-fat cream cheese
¹/₄ to ¹/₃ cup sugar, to taste
1¹/₂ teaspoons WATKINS Vanilla
2 peaches or nectarines, thinly sliced
2 kiwi, peeled and sliced
1 cup fresh strawberries, hulled and sliced
1 cup fresh blueberries
2 tablespoons honey
¹/₂ teaspoon WATKINS Orange Extract
¹/₂ to 1 teaspoon water

Preheat oven to 450°F. Press pastry onto bottom and up side of 10-inch tart pan with removable bottom; trim edges if necessary. Prick crust with fork. Bake for 9 to 11 minutes or until lightly browned. Remove from oven and cool completely.

Combine cream cheese, sugar and vanilla in small bowl; mix well. Spread evenly over cooled tart shell. (At this point, shell may be covered and refrigerated overnight.) Carefully arrange fruit over cream cheese layer. Blend honey, orange extract and enough water to form glaze. Brush glaze over fruit. Refrigerate tart until ready to serve. Remove side of pan before serving. *Makes 10 servings*

Tip: Vary the fruit in the tart by using whatever is on hand or in season in your area.

Fresh Fruit Tart

Brownie Pie à la Mode

$^1/_2$ cup (1 stick) reduced-calorie stick margarine

$^1/_4$ cup WATKINS Pure Cocoa

$^3/_4$ cup sugar

$^3/_4$ cup all-purpose flour

2 egg whites

$1^1/_2$ teaspoons WATKINS Vanilla

1 teaspoon WATKINS Baking Powder

4 cups fat-free frozen yogurt or ice cream

Fresh or thawed frozen berries (optional)

Preheat oven to 350°F. Spray 9-inch pie pan with WATKINS Cooking Spray. Melt margarine in small saucepan over medium heat; stir in cocoa until well blended and smooth. Remove from heat. Stir in sugar, flour, egg whites, vanilla and baking powder; mix well. Spread batter into prepared pan. Bake for 20 minutes or until toothpick inserted into center comes out clean. Cool in pan on wire rack. Cut into 8 wedges; top with frozen yogurt. Garnish with berries, if desired.   *Makes 8 servings*

Brownie Pie à la Mode

Blue Ribbon Cream Pie

$^2/_3$ cup plus $^1/_4$ cup sugar, divided
$^1/_2$ cup WATKINS Vanilla Dessert Mix
$^1/_2$ cup water
2 egg yolks, slightly beaten
$2^1/_2$ cups milk
1 tablespoon WATKINS Vanilla
$1^1/_4$ cups graham cracker crumbs
$^1/_3$ cup melted butter
$^1/_2$ teaspoon WATKINS Ground Cinnamon
1 can (21 ounces) blueberry pie filling
1 teaspoon WATKINS Almond Extract
1 cup sour cream
2 cups Vanilla Whipped Cream (page 35)

Combine $^2/_3$ cup sugar, dessert mix and water in medium saucepan. Beat egg yolks into milk in small bowl; stir into sugar mixture until well blended. Cook over medium heat until mixture begins to boil and thicken. Remove from heat and stir in vanilla. Cover surface with plastic wrap; cool to room temperature.

For crust, preheat oven to 375°F. Combine graham cracker crumbs, melted butter, remaining $^1/_4$ cup sugar and cinnamon in medium bowl; mix well. Spread mixture into 9-inch pie pan; press onto bottom and up side of pan $^1/_2$ inch higher than rim. Bake for 8 minutes; cool on wire rack.

Combine blueberry pie filling and almond extract; spread 1 cup blueberry pie filling over bottom of crust. Stir sour cream into cooled vanilla mixture; spread over blueberry layer. Spoon remaining blueberry pie filling evenly over center of vanilla mixture; refrigerate at least 2 hours. Pipe or dollop Vanilla Whipped Cream over pie before serving.   *Makes 10 servings*

Custard Pie

Pastry for single-crust 9-inch pie

4 eggs, slightly beaten

$^1/_2$ cup sugar

$^1/_4$ teaspoon salt

$2^1/_2$ cups milk, scalded (heated to just below boiling point)

2 teaspoons WATKINS Vanilla

$^1/_8$ teaspoon WATKINS Almond Extract

$^1/_4$ teaspoon WATKINS Nutmeg

Preheat oven to 400°F. Place pastry in pie pan and chill while preparing filling. Blend eggs, sugar and salt in large bowl. Gradually stir in scalded milk. Add extracts; stir until blended. Pour into pastry-lined pie pan; sprinkle with nutmeg. Bake for 25 to 30 minutes or until knife inserted halfway between outside and center comes out clean. Cool on wire rack 30 minutes; refrigerate until completely chilled.   *Makes 10 servings*

Old-Fashioned Pumpkin Pie

1 cup sugar

1 tablespoon all-purpose flour

1 tablespoon WATKINS Pumpkin Pie Spice

$^1/_2$ teaspoon salt

3 large eggs

$1^1/_2$ cups mashed, cooked pumpkin or canned pumpkin

1 cup evaporated milk

1 unbaked 9-inch pie crust

Vanilla Whipped Cream (optional, page 35)

Preheat oven to 400°F. Combine sugar, flour, pumpkin pie spice and salt in large bowl; beat in eggs until well blended. Stir in pumpkin and milk until smooth. Pour into pie crust. Bake for 50 minutes or until knife inserted into center comes out clean. Serve with Vanilla Whipped Cream, if desired. *Makes 10 servings*

Old-Fashioned Pumpkin Pie

Peaches and Cream Pie

$^3/_4$ cup all-purpose flour

$^1/_2$ cup milk

$^1/_3$ cup plus 9 tablespoons sugar, divided

1 egg

$^1/_4$ cup WATKINS Vanilla Dessert Mix

3 tablespoons butter, softened

1 teaspoon WATKINS Baking Powder

$^1/_2$ teaspoon salt

$^1/_4$ teaspoon WATKINS Nutmeg

1 can (16 ounces) sliced peaches, undrained

1 package (8 ounces) cream cheese, softened

$^1/_2$ teaspoon WATKINS Vanilla

$^1/_2$ teaspoon WATKINS Ground Cinnamon

Preheat oven to 350°F. Grease bottom of 9-inch deep-dish pie pan or 10-inch standard pie pan. Combine flour, milk, $^1/_3$ cup sugar, egg, dessert mix, butter, baking powder, salt and nutmeg in large bowl. Beat with electric mixer at medium speed 2 minutes. Pour into prepared pan. Drain peaches, reserving 3 tablespoons juice. Arrange drained peaches over batter, leaving $^1/_2$ to 1 inch batter around edge of pan uncovered.

Combine cream cheese, $^1/_2$ cup sugar, reserved peach juice and vanilla; beat until smooth. Spread over peaches, leaving edge uncovered. Combine remaining 1 tablespoon sugar and cinnamon; sprinkle over cream cheese mixture. Bake for 30 to 45 minutes. Cool to room temperature; chill until ready to serve.   *Makes 10 servings*

Bavarian Apple Tart

CRUST

> $^1/_2$ cup (1 stick) butter, softened
>
> $^1/_3$ cup sugar
>
> $^1/_2$ teaspoon WATKINS Clear Vanilla Extract
>
> 1 cup all-purpose flour
>
> $^1/_8$ teaspoon WATKINS Ground Cinnamon

FILLING

> 1 package (8 ounces) cream cheese
>
> $^1/_4$ cup plus $^1/_3$ cup sugar, divided
>
> 1 egg
>
> $1^1/_2$ teaspoons WATKINS Clear Vanilla Extract
>
> $^3/_4$ teaspoon WATKINS Ground Cinnamon
>
> 4 cups peeled and sliced Granny Smith apples

Preheat oven to 450°F. For crust, beat butter and $^1/_3$ cup sugar in medium bowl until light and fluffy. Add $^1/_2$ teaspoon vanilla; mix well. Add flour and $^1/_8$ teaspoon cinnamon; mix well. Spread onto bottom and 1 inch up side of 9-inch springform pan.

For filling, beat cream cheese and $^1/_4$ cup sugar in small bowl until fluffy. Beat in egg and $1^1/_2$ teaspoons vanilla; spread over crust. Combine remaining $^1/_3$ cup sugar and $^3/_4$ teaspoon cinnamon in large bowl; add apples and toss to coat. Arrange apples in attractive pattern over cream cheese filling. Bake for 10 minutes. Reduce heat to 400°F; bake for 25 minutes. Cool completely. Keep refrigerated.

Makes 8 servings

Fireside French Apple Pie

Pastry for single-crust 10-inch pie
$^3/_4$ cup granulated sugar
$^3/_4$ cup all-purpose flour, divided
2 tablespoons WATKINS Butterscotch Dessert Mix
1$^3/_4$ teaspoons WATKINS Apple Bake Seasoning
$^1/_4$ teaspoon salt
8 cups peeled and thinly sliced tart apples (Greening, Granny
Smith, Rome Beauty or Winesap)
$^1/_2$ cup packed brown sugar
$^1/_2$ cup chopped pecans
$^1/_4$ cup ($^1/_2$ stick) butter
Vanilla Whipped Cream (page 35)

Preheat oven to 400°F. Place pastry in pie pan; trim and flute edge.
Combine granulated sugar, $^1/_4$ cup flour, dessert mix, apple bake seasoning
and salt in large bowl. Add apples; toss to coat. Fill pastry with apple
mixture.

Mix remaining $^1/_2$ cup flour, brown sugar, pecans and butter in small
bowl with fork until crumbly; sprinkle over apple mixture. Cover pie
loosely with foil. Bake on lowest oven rack for 50 to 60 minutes,
removing foil during last 15 minutes of baking time. Serve with
dollop of Vanilla Whipped Cream. *Makes 8 servings*

Fireside French Apple Pie

Irresistible Cookies & Bars

Who can say no to fresh-baked cookies or rich, fudgy brownies? These tasty treats are great for lunch boxes, after-school snacks, holiday gifts or any time you need to satisfy your sweet tooth.

Cookies on a Stick

1 cup sugar

$^1/_2$ cup (1 stick) butter or margarine, softened

1 egg

1 teaspoon WATKINS Vanilla

$^1/_2$ teaspoon WATKINS Butter Extract

1 package (3 ounces) cream cheese, softened

2$^1/_4$ cups all-purpose flour

$^1/_2$ teaspoon WATKINS Baking Powder

$^1/_4$ teaspoon salt

$^1/_8$ teaspoon baking soda

$^1/_4$ cup WATKINS Pure Cocoa

1 teaspoon WATKINS Ground Cinnamon

36 wooden craft sticks

Beat sugar and butter in large bowl until light and fluffy. Add egg and extracts; mix well. Stir in cream cheese until well blended. Combine flour, baking powder, salt and baking soda in small bowl. Stir into butter mixture; blend well. Divide dough in half. Add cocoa to one half of dough, mixing well. Add cinnamon to other half. Cover each half of dough with plastic wrap and chill 15 minutes or until firm enough to roll.

Roll out each half of dough between two sheets of waxed paper into 9-inch square. Place chocolate dough on top of cinnamon dough; roll up jelly-roll fashion. Wrap tightly in plastic wrap; chill several hours or overnight.

Preheat oven to 350°F. Cut roll of dough into $^1/_4$-inch slices; place on ungreased cookie sheets. Insert wooden stick through edge into center of each slice, pressing to hold in place. Bake for 10 to 12 minutes or until lightly browned. Remove from cookie sheets; cool completely on wire racks. *Makes 36 cookies*

Peanut Buster Bar Dessert

2$^1\!/_2$ cups crushed round chocolate sandwich cookies

6 tablespoons butter, softened

2 quarts vanilla ice cream or ice milk, slightly softened

2 cups powdered sugar

1$^1\!/_2$ cups evaporated milk

$^2\!/_3$ cup semisweet chocolate chips

$^1\!/_2$ cup (1 stick) butter

1$^1\!/_2$ teaspoons WATKINS Vanilla

1$^1\!/_2$ cups Spanish peanuts

Mix cookie crumbs and 6 tablespoons softened butter in medium bowl; pat into 13×9-inch baking dish. Chill in freezer until set. Pack ice cream into chocolate crust; return to freezer.

Combine powdered sugar, milk, chocolate chips and $^1\!/_2$ cup butter in medium saucepan; bring to a boil over medium heat, stirring constantly, until melted and smooth. Remove from heat and add vanilla; let sauce cool slightly. Sprinkle peanuts over ice cream; top with chocolate sauce. Return to freezer until frozen. *Makes 18 servings*

Cherry Cheese Squares

$1\frac{1}{4}$ cups all-purpose flour

$\frac{1}{2}$ cup brown sugar

$\frac{1}{2}$ cup vegetable shortening

$\frac{1}{2}$ teaspoon WATKINS Butter Extract

$\frac{1}{2}$ cup flaked coconut

$\frac{1}{2}$ cup finely chopped almonds

2 packages (8 ounces each) cream cheese, softened

$\frac{2}{3}$ cup granulated sugar

2 eggs, beaten

2 teaspoons WATKINS Clear Vanilla Extract

1 to 2 cans (21 ounces each) cherry pie filling*

$\frac{1}{2}$ to 1 teaspoon WATKINS Almond Extract*

$\frac{1}{2}$ cup slivered almonds

*The amount of cherries can be increased to your own personal taste. For more cheesecake flavor, use one can of cherries and $\frac{1}{2}$ teaspoon extract; for a more intense cherry flavor, use 2 cans of cherries and 1 teaspoon extract.

Preheat oven to 350°F. Grease 13×9-inch baking dish. Combine flour and brown sugar; cut in shortening and butter extract until fine crumbs form. Stir in coconut and chopped almonds. Reserve $\frac{1}{2}$ cup mixture for topping. Press remaining mixture into bottom of prepared baking dish. Bake for 12 to 15 minutes or until lightly browned.

Meanwhile, for filling, beat cream cheese, granulated sugar, eggs and vanilla in large bowl until smooth. Spread over hot crust. Bake for 15 minutes. Combine cherry pie filling and almond extract; spread over cream cheese layer. Combine reserved crumbs and slivered almonds; sprinkle over cherry layer. Bake for 15 minutes. Cool on wire rack. Refrigerate until ready to serve.   *Makes 24 servings*

Mother's Old-Fashioned Oatmeal Cookies

1 cup (2 sticks) butter, softened
1 cup granulated sugar
1 cup packed light brown sugar
2 eggs, at room temperature
2 teaspoons WATKINS Vanilla
1 1/4 cups all-purpose flour
1 teaspoon salt
1 teaspoon baking soda
1 teaspoon WATKINS Ground Cinnamon
1/2 teaspoon WATKINS Ground Cloves
1/2 teaspoon WATKINS Allspice
3 cups old-fashioned rolled oats
3/4 cup chopped pecans
Powdered sugar (optional)

Preheat oven to 350°F. Lightly grease cookie sheets. Combine butter, sugars, eggs and vanilla in large bowl; beat until fluffy. Combine flour, salt, baking soda, cinnamon, cloves and allspice in medium bowl; beat into butter mixture until blended. Stir in oats and pecans. Drop by teaspoonfuls onto prepared cookie sheets.

Bake for 10 to 15 minutes. Cool briefly on cookie sheets; remove to wire racks to cool completely. Dust with powdered sugar, if desired.

Makes 6 dozen cookies

$1,000,000 Bars

1 cup (2 sticks) plus 2 tablespoons butter, softened, divided

2 cups packed brown sugar

2 eggs

2 teaspoons WATKINS Vanilla

1 teaspoon WATKINS Almond Extract

2½ cups all-purpose flour

1 teaspoon baking soda

1½ teaspoons salt, divided

3 cups quick-cooking rolled oats

1 package (12 ounces) semisweet chocolate chips

1 can (14 ounces) sweetened condensed milk

1 cup chopped walnuts

2 teaspoons WATKINS Vanilla Nut Extract

Preheat oven to 350°F. Grease 13×9-inch baking pan. Beat 1 cup
butter and brown sugar in large bowl until light and fluffy. Beat in eggs
and extracts. Sift flour, baking soda and 1 teaspoon salt into medium
bowl; stir in oats. Add flour mixture to butter mixture; beat until blended.

Combine chocolate chips, sweetened condensed milk, remaining
2 tablespoons butter and ½ teaspoon salt in medium saucepan; heat
over low heat until chips are melted and mixture is smooth. Stir in
walnuts and vanilla nut extract. Spread half of oat mixture in bottom
of prepared pan. Top with chocolate mixture; drop teaspoonfuls of
remaining oat mixture over top. Bake for 25 to 30 minutes or until
golden brown.   *Makes 48 bars*

Coconut Cream Cheese Brownies

1 cup (2 sticks) butter, melted

4 eggs, divided

1 $^1/_2$ teaspoon WATKINS Vanilla

2 $^1/_4$ cups sugar, divided

1 $^1/_4$ cups all-purpose flour

$^1/_2$ cup WATKINS Pure Cocoa

$^1/_2$ teaspoon WATKINS Baking Powder

$^1/_4$ teaspoon salt

1 cup semisweet chocolate chips

2 packages (8 ounces each) cream cheese

2 teaspoons WATKINS Coconut Extract

$^3/_4$ cup WATKINS Coconut Dessert Mix

2 tablespoons milk

Preheat oven to 350°F. Grease 13×9-inch baking pan with WATKINS Cooking Spray. Blend butter, 3 eggs and vanilla in large bowl. Combine 2 cups sugar, flour, cocoa, baking powder and salt in medium bowl; stir into egg mixture until well blended. Stir in chocolate chips. Set aside half of batter for topping. Spread remaining batter into prepared pan.

Beat cream cheese, remaining $^1/_4$ cup sugar and coconut extract in small bowl until smooth. Add dessert mix, remaining egg and milk; beat just until combined. Carefully spread filling over batter. Drop reserved batter by tablespoonfuls over filling. Cut through batter with knife to swirl, if desired. Bake for 35 to 40 minutes or until toothpick inserted into center comes out clean. Cool in pan on wire rack. Refrigerate until ready to serve. *Makes 3 dozen brownies*

Favorite recipe from **Susan Hurst, Washington**

Coconut Cream Cheese Brownies

"It was a long time ago I started using Watkins"

Delicious Lemon Squares

$^{1}/_{2}$ cup (1 stick) butter, softened

1 cup all-purpose flour

$^{1}/_{2}$ cup chopped pecans

1 teaspoon WATKINS Butter Extract

1 cup powdered sugar

1 package (8 ounces) fat-free or light cream cheese, at room
    temperature

1 teaspoon WATKINS Vanilla

2 cups whipped topping (half of 1-quart container)

1 pie filling recipe WATKINS Lemon Dessert Mix

1 tablespoon lemon juice

Preheat oven to 375°F. Beat butter, flour, pecans and butter extract
in medium bowl until well blended. Press onto bottom of 11×7-inch
baking pan. Bake for 15 minutes; cool completely in pan on wire rack.

Beat powdered sugar, cream cheese and vanilla until smooth. Fold in
whipped topping; set aside. Prepare lemon pie filling according to package
directions with $2^{1}/_{2}$ cups water; stir in lemon juice and cool completely.

Spread thin layer cream cheese mixture over baked crust. Spread lemon
pie filling over cream cheese layer; top with remaining cream cheese
mixture. (Chilling after adding lemon pie filling may make it easier to
spread top layer.) Chill before cutting into squares.   *Makes 15 squares*

Note: Other Watkins Dessert Mixes may be used instead of Lemon.

Favorite recipe from **Rhona O'Hara, New Brunswick**

Mexican Wedding Cakes

1 cup (2 sticks) butter, softened
$^1/_2$ cup powdered sugar, plus additional for dusting cookies
2 teaspoons WATKINS Vanilla
2 cups sifted all-purpose flour
1 cup finely chopped walnuts, almonds or pecans
2 tablespoons half-and-half
WATKINS Ground Cinnamon

Preheat oven to 350°F. Beat butter, $^1/_2$ cup sugar and vanilla in large bowl until light and fluffy. Stir in flour, walnuts and half-and-half; beat until smooth. Shape dough into 1-inch balls; place on ungreased cookie sheets.

Bake for 15 to 20 minutes or until set but not brown. Cool slightly; roll in powdered sugar to coat and set on wire racks to cool. Combine additional powdered sugar with cinnamon to taste. Roll cookies in cinnamon-sugar mixture. Store in airtight containers.

Makes 36 cookies

Biscotti

3 cups all-purpose flour

2 teaspoons WATKINS Baking Powder

$1/2$ teaspoon salt

4 eggs, slightly beaten

1 cup sugar

$1/2$ cup (1 stick) butter, melted

2 teaspoons WATKINS Vanilla

$1\,1/2$ teaspoons WATKINS Almond Extract

$3/4$ cup finely chopped blanched almonds

Preheat oven to 350°F. Combine flour, baking powder and salt in medium bowl. Beat eggs, sugar and melted butter in large bowl; stir in extracts. Add flour mixture, one third at a time; mixing well after each addition. Fold in almonds. Shape dough into two logs, each 12 inches long, 3 inches wide and $1\,1/2$ inches high, on cookie sheet.

Bake for 20 minutes or just until logs begin to brown around edges. Cool 10 minutes. Remove logs from cookie sheet and place on cutting board; cut logs crosswise into $1/2$-inch-thick slices. Lay slices cut sides down on cookie sheet and bake for 12 minutes. Turn cookies over and bake for 5 to 10 minutes or until dry and crisp. *Makes 48 cookies*

Toffee Squares

1 cup (2 sticks) butter, softened
1 cup packed brown sugar
1 tablespoon WATKINS Vanilla
2 cups all-purpose flour
6 milk chocolate bars, unwrapped
1 cup chopped toasted almonds

Preheat oven to 350°F. Beat butter and brown sugar in large bowl until light and fluffy. Add vanilla; gradually beat in flour until smooth and blended. (Dough will be stiff.) Pat evenly into ungreased 15×10-inch jelly-roll pan. Bake for 25 to 30 minutes or until crust is golden.

Remove from oven; arrange chocolate bars evenly over top of crust and let stand 5 minutes to soften. Spread chocolate evenly over crust; sprinkle with almonds. Cool before cutting into squares.

Makes 40 squares

Note: This recipe produces a crunchy bottom crust. For a softer version, add one egg along with the vanilla and reduce the baking time to 18 to 20 minutes.

Holiday Spice Prints

1 cup packed dark brown sugar

$^3/_4$ cup (1$^1/_2$ sticks) butter, softened

1 egg

$^1/_4$ cup molasses

1 teaspoon WATKINS Vanilla

2$^1/_2$ cups all-purpose flour

2 teaspoons baking soda

2 teaspoons WATKINS Ginger

1 teaspoon WATKINS Ground Cinnamon

$^3/_4$ teaspoon WATKINS Ground Cloves

$^1/_2$ teaspoon WATKINS Allspice

$^1/_4$ teaspoon salt (optional)

Granulated sugar

Beat brown sugar and butter in large bowl until creamy. Beat in egg, molasses and vanilla. Combine flour, baking soda, spices and salt, if desired. Stir into butter mixture until well blended. Chill dough for 1 hour.

Preheat oven to 375°F. Grease cookie sheets. Place granulated sugar in shallow bowl. Roll dough into 1$^1/_2$-inch balls; dip tops in granulated sugar. Place balls, sugar side up, about 3 inches apart on prepared cookie sheets. Bake for 10 to 12 minutes or until set but not hard. Firmly press top of each cookie with clay stamp or wooden butter mold immediately after removing from oven. Pierce top of each cookie with drinking straw to make hole for hanging, if desired. Transfer to wire racks to cool completely. When cool, thread each cookie with ribbon for hanging.

Makes 5 dozen cookies

Watkins Cocoa Brownies

3/4 cup (1 1/2 sticks) butter, divided

1 cup granulated sugar

2 eggs

2 teaspoons WATKINS Vanilla, divided

1/3 cup plus 1/4 cup WATKINS Pure Cocoa, divided

1/2 cup all-purpose flour

1/4 teaspoon salt

1/4 teaspoon WATKINS Baking Powder

1 cup powdered sugar

1 tablespoons light corn syrup or honey

Preheat oven to 350°F. Spray 8-inch square baking pan with WATKINS Cooking Spray and dust with flour. Melt 1/2 cup butter in large saucepan. Remove from heat; stir in granulated sugar, eggs and 1 teaspoon vanilla. Beat in 1/3 cup cocoa, flour, salt and baking powder. Spread batter into prepared pan. Bake for 25 to 30 minutes.

Meanwhile, combine powdered sugar, remaining 1/4 cup cocoa, 1/4 cup butter, 1 teaspoon vanilla and corn syrup in medium bowl; beat until well blended and smooth. Frost brownies while still warm.

Makes 16 brownies

Old-Fashioned Spice Bars

    1 cup raisins
    1 cup hot water
    1/2 cup WATKINS Original Grapeseed Oil
    1 cup granulated sugar
    1 egg
1 3/4 cups flour
    1 teaspoon baking soda
    1 teaspoon WATKINS Ground Cinnamon
    1/2 teaspoon WATKINS Nutmeg
    1/2 teaspoon WATKINS Allspice
    1/2 teaspoon WATKINS Ground Cloves
    1/4 teaspoon salt
    1/2 cup chopped walnuts or other nuts
    3 cups powdered sugar
    1/2 cup vegetable shortening
    1 teaspoon WATKINS Vanilla
    Milk

Preheat oven to 350°F. Spray 15×10-inch jelly-roll pan with
WATKINS Cooking Spray. Combine raisins and hot water in medium
saucepan; bring to a boil. Remove from heat, stir in oil and set aside
to plump raisins.

Combine granulated sugar and egg in large bowl; blend until smooth.
Sift flour, baking soda, spices and salt into medium bowl; beat into sugar
mixture. Stir in raisin mixture and walnuts. Pour batter into prepared pan.

Bake for 15 to 20 minutes; cool slightly in pan on wire rack. Meanwhile, beat powdered sugar and shortening in medium bowl with electric mixer until well blended. Add vanilla and milk, 1 teaspoon at a time; beat at medium-low speed until icing is of spreading consistency. Spread over bars while still warm but not hot. *Makes 48 bars*

Old-Fashioned Spice Bars

Two-Tone Swirls

$^3/_4$ cup (1$^1/_2$ sticks) butter, softened

1$^1/_4$ cups sugar

2 eggs

3 cups all-purpose flour

1 teaspoon WATKINS Baking Powder

$^1/_2$ teaspoon salt

1 teaspoon WATKINS Vanilla

1 tablespoon WATKINS Chocolate Dessert Mix

1 teaspoon WATKINS Almond Extract

1 teaspoon WATKINS Chocolate Extract

Beat butter in large bowl with electric mixer until smooth. Gradually add sugar and beat until well blended. Add eggs; beat until light and fluffy. Stir in flour, baking powder and salt. Remove half of dough to another bowl. Add vanilla to one half; fold dessert mix and extracts into other half. Cover each dough; refrigerate for 1$^1/_2$ to 2 hours.

Roll each dough into 12×8-inch rectangle on lightly floured surface; cut each rectangle in half to form two 8×6-inch rectangles. Place one chocolate layer on top of one vanilla layer, lining up long edges. Starting with short side, roll to center jelly-roll fashion. Turn over and roll other half to center, forming "S" shape. Repeat with remaining dough. Wrap rolls tightly in plastic wrap; chill in freezer for about 1$^1/_2$ hours or until very firm.

Preheat oven to 375°F. Grease cookie sheets. Cut dough into $^1/_4$-inch slices; place about $^1/_2$ inch apart on prepared cookie sheets. Bake for 9 to 10 minutes or until edges begin to brown. Let stand on cookie sheets 1 minute; transfer to wire racks to cool completely.

Makes 42 cookies

White Chocolate Chip Brownies

  1 cup vanilla milk chips

$^{1}/_{4}$ cup ($^{1}/_{2}$ stick) butter

  2 eggs

$^{1}/_{2}$ cup sugar

  1 teaspoon WATKINS Vanilla

$^{1}/_{2}$ teaspoon WATKINS Almond Extract

  1 cup all-purpose flour

$^{1}/_{4}$ teaspoon WATKINS Baking Powder

$^{1}/_{4}$ teaspoon WATKINS Nutmeg

  1 cup semisweet mini chocolate chips

$^{1}/_{2}$ cup chopped macadamia nuts or toasted almonds

$^{1}/_{4}$ cup semisweet chocolate chips

  1 teaspoon vegetable shortening

Preheat oven to 350°F. Grease 11×7-inch baking dish. Melt vanilla chips and butter in small saucepan over low heat; set aside to cool slightly. Beat eggs, sugar and extracts in large bowl with electric mixer at high speed for 2 minutes. Beat in vanilla chip mixture at low speed until well blended. Stir in flour, baking powder and nutmeg; mix well. Stir in mini chocolate chips and macadamia nuts. Spread into prepared baking dish.

Bake for 25 to 30 minutes or until top is light brown and center is set. Cool completely on wire rack. For glaze, melt chocolate chips and shortening in microwave or in small saucepan over low heat; stir until smooth. Drizzle over top of brownies. Let glaze set before cutting into bars.   *Makes 24 brownies*

Dream Bars

1 cup (2 sticks) butter, divided
$^1/_4$ cup WATKINS Pure Cocoa
2 teaspoons WATKINS Vanilla
2 cups graham cracker crumbs
3$^1/_2$ cups powdered sugar, divided
$^1/_2$ cup flaked coconut
$^1/_2$ cup chopped walnuts
2 tablespoons water
2 teaspoons WATKINS Ground Cinnamon
$^1/_2$ cup butter or margarine
$^1/_2$ cup milk
$^1/_2$ cup WATKINS Vanilla Dessert Mix
1 bar (8 ounces) milk chocolate, cut into pieces

Grease 13×9-inch baking pan. Melt $^1/_2$ cup butter with cocoa in medium saucepan over low heat, stirring occasionally. Remove from heat and add vanilla; mix well. Stir in graham cracker crumbs, $^1/_2$ cup powdered sugar, coconut, walnuts, water and cinnamon; mix well. Press mixture onto bottom of prepared pan. Refrigerate crust.

Melt remaining $^1/_2$ cup butter in medium saucepan over low heat. Blend in milk and dessert mix. Cook, stirring constantly, about 5 minutes or until mixture thickens slightly. Remove from heat; beat in remaining 3 cups powdered sugar until smooth. Spread over chilled crust. Refrigerate for 20 to 30 minutes or until set.

Melt chocolate in small saucepan over low heat, stirring constantly. Spread evenly over filling. Refrigerate for 10 to 15 minutes until chocolate is set. Cut into squares; store in refrigerator.   *Makes 36 bars*

Macaroons

4 egg whites

²/₃ cup sugar

¹/₄ cup all-purpose flour

1 tablespoon WATKINS Vanilla

Dash salt

2 cups shredded coconut

¹/₄ teaspoon dried orange peel

Preheat oven to 325°F. Grease and flour two large cookie sheets. Beat egg whites lightly in medium bowl. Add sugar, flour, vanilla and salt; mix well. Stir in coconut and orange peel. Drop dough by tablespoonfuls 2 inches apart onto prepared cookie sheets.

Bake both cookie sheets at one time (on two racks) for 13 to 17 minutes or until set and lightly browned, alternating cookie sheets from top to bottom and front to back after 6 minutes. Immediately remove cookies to wire racks to cool.   *Makes 2 dozen cookies*

Mint Cream Cheese Brownies

1 cup plus 3 tablespoons sugar, divided

2/3 cup WATKINS Pure Cocoa

1/3 cup plus 1 tablespoon all-purpose flour, divided

1/2 teaspoon WATKINS Baking Powder

5 egg whites, divided

1/4 cup WATKINS Original Grapeseed Oil

1 1/2 teaspoons WATKINS Vanilla, divided

3/4 teaspoon WATKINS Peppermint Extract, divided

6 ounces fat-free cream cheese

Preheat oven to 350°F. Spray 8-inch square baking pan with WATKINS Cooking Spray. Combine 1 cup sugar, cocoa, 1/3 cup flour and baking powder in large bowl; mix well. Beat 4 egg whites lightly in small bowl; beat in oil, 1 teaspoon vanilla and 1/2 teaspoon peppermint extract. Add to dry ingredients; mix well. Spread batter into prepared pan.

Beat cream cheese, remaining 3 tablespoons sugar, 1 tablespoon flour, 1 egg white, 1/2 teaspoon vanilla and 1/4 teaspoon peppermint extract in medium bowl with electric mixer at low speed until smooth. Spoon cream cheese mixture by tablespoonfuls over batter. Cut through layers with knife to marble. Bake for 22 minutes or until toothpick inserted into center comes out almost clean. Cool in pan on wire rack.   *Makes 16 brownies*

Nanaimo Bars

1 cup (2 sticks) butter, divided

2 1/4 cups powdered sugar, divided

1/4 cup WATKINS Pure Cocoa

4 teaspoons WATKINS Vanilla, divided

1 large egg

1 3/4 cups graham cracker crumbs

1 cup sweetened flaked coconut

1/2 cup chopped pecans or walnuts

2 tablespoons milk

3 squares (1 ounce) semisweet chocolate

Preheat oven to 350°F. Combine 6 tablespoons butter, 1/4 cup powdered sugar and cocoa in large saucepan. Cook over low heat, stirring frequently, until butter is melted. Remove from heat; stir in 1 teaspoon vanilla and egg until well blended. Stir in graham cracker crumbs, coconut and pecans. Press mixture firmly onto bottom of 8-inch square baking dish. Bake for 20 minutes; remove pan to wire rack to cool.

Beat 1/2 cup butter, remaining 2 cups powdered sugar, 1 tablespoon vanilla and milk until light and fluffy. Spread over crust. Melt chocolate and remaining 2 tablespoons butter in microwave or in small saucepan over low heat; stir until smooth. Spread over filling. Cover and chill for at least 1 hour before cutting into squares. *Makes 24 squares*

Lemon Tea Cookies

1 cup (2 sticks) plus 1 tablespoon butter or margarine, softened
$^3/_4$ cup sugar, divided
$2^1/_4$ cups all-purpose flour
1 egg
1 teaspoon WATKINS Vanilla
$^1/_2$ teaspoon WATKINS Butter Extract
$^1/_2$ teaspoon salt
$^1/_2$ cup water
1 egg, beaten
2 tablespoons WATKINS Lemon Dessert Mix
1 teaspoon WATKINS Lemon Extract
Toasted coconut for garnish

Beat 1 cup butter and $^1/_2$ cup sugar in large bowl with electric mixer until light and fluffy. Stir in flour, egg, vanilla, butter extract and salt; mix well. Chill 30 minutes. Preheat oven to 400°F. Shape dough into 1-inch balls; use thumb or forefinger to make an imprint in center of each ball. Place on ungreased cookie sheet and bake for 6 to 9 minutes until set but not brown. Remove to wire racks to cool completely.

Combine water, beaten egg, dessert mix, remaining $^1/_4$ cup sugar and 1 tablespoon butter in medium saucepan. Cook over medium heat, stirring constantly, until smooth and thickened. Remove from heat; stir in lemon extract. Spoon $^1/_4$ teaspoon lemon filling onto center of each cookie. Sprinkle with coconut. *Makes 36 cookies*

Lemon Tea Cookies

Extraordinary Desserts

Cookies and cakes are great, but
sometimes you want a little change of
pace—how about a flan, mousse or
truffles? Simple or sophisticated, these
desserts will make a lasting impression!

Blueberry Cobbler

4 cups fresh or thawed frozen blueberries

$^1/_2$ teaspoon WATKINS Lemon Extract

1 cup all-purpose flour

$^1/_2$ cup plus 2 tablespoons sugar, divided

1 teaspoon WATKINS Baking Powder

Dash salt

2 egg whites, lightly beaten

1 tablespoon WATKINS Original Grapeseed Oil

1 teaspoon WATKINS Vanilla

$^1/_4$ teaspoon WATKINS Ground Cinnamon or more to taste

Preheat oven to 350°F. Spray 1$^1/_2$-quart baking dish with WATKINS Cooking Spray. Add blueberries and lemon extract to dish; toss lightly. Combine flour, $^1/_2$ cup sugar, baking powder and salt in medium bowl; mix well. Beat egg whites, oil and vanilla in small bowl until well blended. Make well in center of dry ingredients; add egg white mixture and stir just until moistened.

Drop 8 equal mounds of dough onto blueberries. Combine remaining 2 tablespoons sugar and cinnamon; sprinkle over top. Bake for 35 minutes or until bubbly and browned. *Makes 8 servings*

Old-Fashioned Taffy

3 cups sugar

1 1/4 cups boiling water

1/4 cup (1/2 stick) butter

2 tablespoons white vinegar

1 teaspoon WATKINS Vanilla

1/4 to 1 teaspoon favorite WATKINS Extract

Few drops food coloring (optional)

Butter 13×9-inch pan or large platter. Combine sugar, water, butter and vinegar in medium saucepan; bring to a boil, stirring occasionally. Cook over medium heat, without stirring, until mixture reaches 260°F on candy thermometer (hard-ball stage). Remove from heat; stir in vanilla, any other extract of choice and food coloring, if desired.

Pour into prepared pan. Turn mixture toward center with spatula as edges firm. When cool enough to handle, pull taffy with lightly buttered hands until satiny, light in color and stiff. Stretch into long strips 1/2 inch wide. Cut into 1-inch pieces with scissors. Wrap pieces individually in waxed paper. (Candy must be wrapped to hold its shape.)

Makes about 100 pieces

Vanilla Soda

1 ½ teaspoons sugar or equivalent artificial sweetener
1 teaspoon WATKINS Vanilla
1 cup club soda
1 scoop vanilla ice cream

Combine sugar and vanilla in bottom of tall glass; mix well. Pour in club soda, stirring gently to blend. Carefully add ice cream to glass; serve with straw and long spoon. *Makes 1 serving*

Mixed Nut Toffee Roll

1 $^1/_4$ cups sugar

$^3/_4$ cup dark corn syrup

$^3/_4$ cup chunky peanut butter

1 teaspoon WATKINS Vanilla

1 teaspoon WATKINS Vanilla Nut Extract

1 can (8 ounces) unsalted or salted dry-roasted mixed nuts

1 cup chopped unsalted or salted dry-roasted peanuts

Grease 13×9-inch baking dish; set aside. Cook sugar and corn syrup in heavy medium saucepan over medium heat, stirring constantly, until sugar is dissolved and mixture begins to boil. Boil 1 minute, stirring constantly. Remove from heat; stir in peanut butter and extracts. Stir until completely blended; stir in mixed nuts only.

Pour into prepared pan; let stand until cool enough to handle. Divide mixture in half; shape each half into log 12 inches long and about 1 $^1/_2$ inches in diameter. Roll logs in chopped peanuts to coat completely. Wrap logs tightly in plastic wrap to hold shape; refrigerate about 1 $^1/_2$ hours or until firm. Cut into $^3/_8$-inch-thick slices with sharp knife. Store slices between waxed paper in tightly covered container in cool, dry place.

Makes 60 pieces

Cinnamon Flan

1 cup sugar, divided
1 teaspoon WATKINS Ground Cinnamon
7 eggs
$^1/_2$ cup cold milk (not low-fat)
1 tablespoon WATKINS Vanilla
    Pinch salt
4 cups hot milk (not low-fat)

Preheat oven to 325°F. Sprinkle $^1/_2$ cup sugar evenly over bottom of heavy small skillet. Cook slowly over low heat, stirring occasionally with wooden spoon, just until sugar melts into golden syrup. Immediately pour syrup into bottom of $1^1/_2$-quart round casserole, turning to coat bottom and as much of side as possible (caramel syrup will harden quickly). Sprinkle with cinnamon and let cool.

Whisk eggs, remaining $^1/_2$ cup sugar, cold milk, vanilla and salt in large bowl. Stir in hot milk; mix well. Pour mixture into caramel-coated casserole. Place casserole in larger baking pan and fill with hot water to depth of 1 inch. Bake for 70 to 80 minutes or until knife inserted into center comes out clean.

Remove casserole from hot water and place on wire rack to cool completely, then refrigerate for at least 1 hour to chill. Just before serving, invert flan into shallow bowl. Cut into slices and spoon some of caramel sauce from bottom of bowl over each serving.   *Makes 8 servings*

Marbled Terrine

VANILLA LAYER

1 1/4 teaspoons unflavored gelatin

2 1/2 cups milk, divided

  1/2 cup Vanilla Dessert Mix

  1/3 cup sugar

  1/3 cup vanilla milk chips

   1 teaspoon WATKINS Vanilla

CHOCOLATE LAYER

1 1/4 teaspoons unflavored gelatin

2 1/2 cups milk, divided

  1/2 cup Chocolate Dessert Mix

  1/2 cup sugar

  1/3 cup semisweet chocolate chips

   1 teaspoon WATKINS Vanilla

   1 cup Vanilla Whipped Cream (page 35)

    Chocolate curls (optional)

Line 8×4-inch loaf pan with plastic wrap; smooth out all wrinkles. For vanilla layer, combine gelatin and 1 cup milk in medium saucepan; let stand 2 minutes or until softened. Add remaining milk, dessert mix and sugar. Cook over medium heat, stirring constantly, until mixture comes to a full boil. Remove from heat; stir in vanilla chips and vanilla until well blended. Cover with plastic (wrap should lay directly on top of mixture to prevent skin from forming) and let stand 15 minutes to cool. Meanwhile, repeat process for chocolate layer.

To assemble terrine, layer half of vanilla mixture in prepared pan; top with half of chocolate mixture. Repeat layers. Gently swirl through mixtures with narrow spatula or knife to marble. Cover with plastic wrap and refrigerate for at least 3 hours before serving. Unmold onto serving plate; remove plastic wrap. Garnish with Vanilla Whipped Cream and chocolate curls, if desired. To serve, cut into slices. Keep refrigerated.

Makes 12 servings

Vanilla Ice Cream

1 can (14 ounces) sweetened condensed milk
$^1/_2$ cup egg substitute
2 tablespoons water
4 teaspoons WATKINS Vanilla*
2 cups heavy whipping cream, whipped

Substitute other Watkins extracts for Vanilla, if desired. Amounts may have to be adjusted for each.

Combine condensed milk, egg substitute, water and vanilla in medium bowl; mix well. Fold mixture into whipped cream. Transfer to plastic container, cover and freeze for at least 6 hours or overnight.

Makes about 6 cups

Simple and Delicious Peach Cobbler

COBBLER

    2 cans (21 ounces each) peach pie filling

    $^1/_2$ cup granulated sugar

    $^3/_4$ teaspoon WATKINS Ground Cinnamon

    $^1/_4$ teaspoon WATKINS Nutmeg

    1 can (10 ounces) refrigerated flaky biscuit dough

    $^1/_4$ cup ($^1/_2$ stick) butter, melted

VANILLA WHIPPED CREAM

    1 cup heavy whipping cream

    2 to 4 tablespoons powdered sugar

    1 teaspoon WATKINS Vanilla

For cobbler, preheat oven to 400°F. Place peach pie filling in 13×9-inch baking dish. Combine granulated sugar, cinnamon and nutmeg in small bowl. Separate each biscuit into 2 sections. Dip each section into butter; roll in sugar mixture to coat. Arrange on top of peach layer. Bake for 20 to 25 minutes or until golden brown.

Meanwhile, prepare whipped cream. Chill small bowl and beaters of electric mixer. Beat cream in chilled bowl until it begins to thicken. Add powdered sugar and vanilla; beat until stiff peaks form. (Do not overbeat.) Serve cobbler warm with whipped cream. *Makes 10 servings*

Note: Cherry or blueberry pie filling may be substituted for peach.

Simple and Delicious Peach Cobbler

Egg Custard

1 1/4 cups whole milk

2 teaspoons WATKINS Vanilla

4 large eggs

1/3 cup granulated sugar

1/8 teaspoon salt

2 tablespoons light brown sugar

1/8 teaspoon WATKINS Ground Cinnamon

Combine milk and vanilla in 4-cup glass measure. Microwave at HIGH for 2 to 3 minutes or until hot but not boiling. Beat eggs, granulated sugar and salt in medium bowl until blended. Gradually whisk in hot milk mixture in slow steady stream, stirring constantly. Pour into six 6-ounce custard cups. Place cups on 10-inch round microwavable plate. Place plate on inverted saucer in microwave oven.

Microwave at MEDIUM (50% power) for 6 to 10 minutes or until edges of custards are set but center is still jiggly, rotating each cup and plate half turn halfway through cooking time. Check for doneness after 5 minutes, then check every 30 seconds and remove each custard cup from microwave when set. Let stand at least 5 minutes or until centers are firm. Combine brown sugar and cinnamon; sprinkle over custards.

Makes 6 servings

Note: If a less sweet dessert is desired, eliminate the cinnamon-sugar topping and sprinkle with Watkins Nutmeg instead.

Low-Fat Vanilla Ice Milk

2 cups 2% low-fat milk

1 cup evaporated skim milk

³/₄ cup egg substitute, thawed if frozen

³/₄ cup sugar

2 to 3 teaspoons WATKINS Vanilla

Combine all ingredients in medium bowl; mix until well blended and sugar is dissolved. Cover and chill for 2 hours or longer. Pour mixture into freezer container of 2-quart hand-cranked or electric ice cream freezer. Freeze according to manufacturer's instructions. Spoon frozen mixture into freezer-safe container; cover and freeze for at least 1 hour before serving. *Makes 8 servings*

Cream Cheese Chantilly

2 packages (3 ounces each) cream cheese, softened

6 tablespoons sugar

2 teaspoons WATKINS Vanilla

1¹/₂ cups heavy whipping cream

Combine cream cheese, sugar and vanilla in medium bowl; beat until smooth. Slowly add cream; beat until light and fluffy. Serve as dessert topping over fresh fruit or cake slices. Refrigerate for up to 3 days.

Makes 2 cups

Creamy Vanilla Mousse with Blueberry Sauce

2$\frac{1}{2}$ cups fresh or frozen blueberries

$\frac{1}{2}$ cup sugar, divided

$\frac{1}{4}$ cup water

1 tablespoon WATKINS Vanilla Dessert Mix

$\frac{1}{8}$ teaspoon WATKINS Almond Extract, more or less as desired

1 envelope unflavored gelatin

$\frac{3}{4}$ cup plus 2 tablespoons skim milk

4 ounces reduced-fat cream cheese, softened

1 carton (8 ounces) nonfat vanilla yogurt

2 teaspoons WATKINS Vanilla

Coat six ($\frac{1}{2}$-cup) molds or one 3-cup mold with WATKINS Cooking Spray. Combine blueberries, $\frac{1}{4}$ cup sugar, water and dessert mix in medium saucepan. Cook over medium heat, stirring constantly, 4 to 5 minutes or until sugar dissolves and mixture beings to boil and thicken. Remove from heat and let cool slightly; stir in almond extract. Cover and chill thoroughly.

Sprinkle gelatin over milk in small saucepan; let stand 1 minute. Cook mixture over low heat, stirring constantly, until gelatin dissolves. Remove pan from heat; set aside and let cool. Place cream cheese in large bowl; beat with electric mixer until smooth. Add yogurt, remaining $\frac{1}{4}$ cup sugar and vanilla; beat until well blended. Add gelatin mixture; beat until smooth.

Spoon into prepared molds; cover and chill until firm. Unmold mousse onto serving plates; serve with blueberry sauce.   *Makes 6 servings*

Creamy Vanilla Mousse with Blueberry Sauce

Vanilla Poached Apples with Ginger Whipped Cream

2 cups sugar

2 cups water

1 tablespoon WATKINS Clear Vanilla Extract

$^1/_4$ teaspoon salt

8 medium Golden Delicious apples, peeled and cored

Ginger Whipped Cream (recipe follows)

Toasted sliced almonds for garnish

Bring sugar and water to a boil in large kettle or Dutch oven. Reduce heat and simmer, uncovered, for 5 minutes. Add vanilla and salt; mix well. Place apples in sugar syrup; cover and simmer for 20 minutes or until tender but not soft, turning apples frequently. Remove apples from syrup; cover and chill overnight.

Prepare Ginger Whipped Cream and spoon into pastry bag fitted with star tip; pipe into centers and on tops of apples. (If desired, apples can be cut into quarters, cutting almost to but not through bottom before topping with Ginger Whipped Cream. This will create "fanning" effect and will make apples easier to eat.) Garnish with almonds.   *Makes 8 servings*

Ginger Whipped Cream

1 cup heavy whipping cream

$^{1}/_{4}$ cup sugar

1 teaspoon WATKINS Ginger

1 teaspoon WATKINS Clear Vanilla Extract

Beat whipping cream in medium bowl with electric mixer until foamy. Gradually add sugar and ginger, beating until soft peaks form. Fold in vanilla.   *Makes 2 cups*

Microwave Caramels

1 pound (2$^{1}/_{4}$ cups) brown sugar

1 cup (2 sticks) butter, melted

1 can (14 ounces) sweetened condensed milk

1 cup light corn syrup

1 tablespoon WATKINS Vanilla

Butter 13×9-inch baking dish. Combine brown sugar, butter, condensed milk and corn syrup in medium microwavable bowl. Microwave at HIGH for 17 minutes, stirring every 5 minutes. Remove from microwave; stir in vanilla. Pour into prepared baking dish; cool. When set, cut into squares and wrap individually in waxed paper. Store in refrigerator.

Makes 116 (1-inch) pieces

Baked Rice Custard

4 cups milk, divided

¾ cup WATKINS Rice Pudding Dessert Mix

1 cup raisins

3 eggs, beaten

⅓ to ½ cup sugar

2½ teaspoons WATKINS Vanilla

⅛ teaspoon WATKINS Nutmeg

WATKINS Ground Cinnamon

Preheat oven to 350°F. Butter 6-cup soufflé dish or casserole. Combine 3 cups milk and dessert mix in heavy medium saucepan; bring to a boil, stirring constantly. Combine remaining 1 cup milk, raisins, eggs, sugar, vanilla and nutmeg in small bowl; gradually stir mixture into saucepan until well blended. Pour into prepared dish; sprinkle lightly with cinnamon. Place dish in large, shallow baking pan; add water to depth of 1 inch.

Bake, uncovered, for about 1 hour and 15 minutes or until knife inserted near center comes out clean. Remove soufflé dish from hot water. Serve custard warm or cold. Refrigerate leftovers. *Makes 10 servings*

Chocolate Fudge

2½ cups sugar
½ cup (1 stick) butter or margarine
1 can (5 ounces) evaporated milk (⅔ cup)
1 jar (7 ounces) marshmallow creme (2 cups)
1 package (12 ounces) semisweet chocolate chips
½ cup chopped walnuts
1 teaspoon WATKINS Vanilla
1 teaspoon WATKINS Vanilla Nut Extract

Line 9-inch square baking pan with foil so foil extends over sides of pan; spray foil with WATKINS Cooking Spray. Combine sugar, butter and evaporated milk in large saucepan; bring to a boil over medium heat, stirring constantly. Continue boiling for 5 minutes, stirring constantly; remove from heat. Stir in marshmallow creme and chocolate chips; blend until smooth. Stir in walnuts and extracts. Pour into prepared pan; cool to room temperature.

Score fudge into 48 squares. Refrigerate until firm. Remove fudge from pan by lifting foil; carefully peel off foil. Cut through scored lines with knife. Store in airtight container in refrigerator with waxed paper between layers. *Makes 48 pieces*

Peanut Fudge: Substitute ½ cup finely chopped peanuts and 2 teaspoons WATKINS Peanut Butter Extract for the walnuts and Vanilla Nut Extract.

Cinnamon Meringue Shells

3 egg whites, at room temperature

1 teaspoon WATKINS Vanilla

$^1/_4$ teaspoon cream of tartar

   Dash salt

$^3/_4$ cup sugar

$^1/_2$ teaspoon WATKINS Ground Cinnamon

Preheat oven to 250°F. Line baking sheet with parchment paper. Beat egg whites, vanilla, cream of tartar and salt until soft peaks form. Combine sugar and cinnamon; add gradually to egg white mixture, beating until very stiff peaks form.

Shape meringue mixture into shells about $3^1/_2$ inches in diameter on prepared baking sheet, using back of spoon to shape into shells. Bake for 30 minutes to 1 hour, then turn off heat and let dry in oven for 1 hour. Carefully remove shells from parchment paper and place on serving plates. Fill with sherbet or sorbet and top with fresh fruit, if desired.   *Makes 8 to 10 shells*

Note: Meringue can be formed into one large shell instead of individual shells. Meringues can be made ahead and stored in an airtight container. They will become soft in humid weather.

Cinnamon Meringue Shells

Vanilla Creme with Strawberries

3 1/2 cups heavy whipping cream or half-and-half

3 cups sour cream

1 1/2 cups plus 2 tablespoons sugar, divided

2 envelopes unflavored gelatin

2 to 3 teaspoons WATKINS Clear Vanilla Extract

1/2 teaspoon WATKINS Banana Extract

4 cups fresh strawberries, divided

1/2 teaspoon WATKINS Strawberry Extract

Combine whipping cream, sour cream, 1 1/2 cups sugar and gelatin in medium saucepan; stir to blend. Cook over low heat, whisking occasionally, for 12 to 15 minutes or until gelatin is dissolved. Add vanilla and banana extract; mix well. Pour into greased 8-cup mold. Chill for 5 to 6 hours or until mixture is set.

Wash and remove stems from 3 cups berries. Place in bowl with remaining 2 tablespoons sugar and strawberry extract; stir to blend and crush berries. Chill until ready to serve. Wash and dry remaining 1 cup berries; chill. Just before serving, unmold gelatin mixture onto serving platter and garnish with whole berries. To serve, spoon onto dessert plates and drizzle with crushed berries. *Makes 10 servings*

Microwave Peanut Brittle

1 1/2 cups unsalted dry-roasted peanuts

1 cup sugar

1/2 cup light corn syrup

1/8 teaspoon salt

1 tablespoon butter

1 tablespoon WATKINS Vanilla

1 tablespoon WATKINS Vanilla Nut Extract

1 teaspoon baking soda

Lightly grease large baking sheet; set aside. Combine peanuts, sugar, corn syrup and salt in large glass mixing bowl. Microwave at HIGH for 7 to 9 minutes until mixture is bubbling and peanuts are brown. Quickly stir in butter and extracts. Microwave at HIGH for 2 to 3 minutes longer. Add baking soda; stir quickly just until mixture is foamy.

Immediately pour mixture onto prepared baking sheet, spreading to desired thickness. Let cool about 15 minutes or until firm. Break peanut brittle into pieces; store in airtight containers.

Makes 1 1/4 pounds

White Chocolate Truffles

2 cups vanilla milk chips
$^1/_4$ cup sour cream
1 $^1/_2$ teaspoons WATKINS Vanilla
$^1/_4$ to $^1/_2$ teaspoon WATKINS Almond Extract
Powdered sugar, cocoa or melted semisweet chocolate

Melt vanilla chips in small saucepan over low heat, stirring constantly; remove from heat. Stir in sour cream and extracts; mix well. (If mixture begins to stiffen, return to low heat until mixture is smooth.)

Refrigerate for about 60 minutes or until mixture is firm enough to handle, stirring occasionally. Shape mixture into $^3/_4$-inch balls. Roll some balls in powdered sugar, some in cocoa or leave plain and pipe melted chocolate in decorative pattern on top with decorating bag. Store in airtight container in refrigerator. *Makes 60 truffles*

Vanilla Glaze

1 $^1/_2$ cups powdered sugar
1 tablespoon butter, softened
$^1/_2$ teaspoon WATKINS Clear Vanilla Extract
$^1/_8$ teaspoon salt (optional)
2 $^1/_2$ tablespoons half-and-half, or more if desired

Combine sugar, butter, vanilla and salt, if desired, in small bowl; add enough half-and-half to reach desired glaze consistency. Use for cakes, cookies or quick breads. *Makes $^3/_4$ cup*

Divinity

2$^1\!/_2$ cups sugar
$^1\!/_2$ cup light corn syrup
$^1\!/_2$ cup water
$^1\!/_4$ teaspoon salt
2 egg whites
2 teaspoons WATKINS Clear Vanilla Extract
Chopped nuts (optional)

Combine sugar, corn syrup, water and salt in heavy medium saucepan. Heat over medium heat, stirring until sugar dissolves. Cover until mixture begins to boil. Remove cover and boil, without stirring, until mixture reaches 260°F (hard-ball stage). Just before syrup reaches this level, beat egg whites with electric mixer until stiff.

Pour syrup slowly over beaten egg whites while beating with electric mixer at high speed. Add vanilla; continue beating for 4 to 5 minutes or until mixture begins to thicken and hold its shape. Add nuts, if desired, and quickly drop by teaspoonfuls onto buttered waxed paper. Let stand until cool. Store in airtight containers. *Makes about 40 pieces*

Variations: For different flavors of divinity, try substituting 2 teaspoons Watkins Strawberry Extract for the Clear Vanilla, or substitute 1 teaspoon Watkins Cherry Extract and chopped well-drained maraschino cherries for the Clear Vanilla and nuts, or add 1 teaspoon Watkins Orange Extract and grated orange peel.

Quick and Easy Mini Fruit Pizzas

1 package (3 ounces) cream cheese

1 tablespoon sugar

$^1/_2$ teaspoon WATKINS Clear Vanilla Extract

$^1/_8$ teaspoon WATKINS Almond Extract

6 store-bought sugar cookies

   Assorted fruit such as strawberries, mandarin oranges, bananas, blueberries and kiwis

   WATKINS Ground Cinnamon

Place cream cheese in small microwavable bowl. Microwave at HIGH for 30 to 45 seconds or until softened. Stir in sugar and extracts. Spread mixture on cookies. Arrange fruit over cream cheese layer. Sprinkle lightly with cinnamon. *Makes 6 servings*

Watkins Cocoa Ice Cream

1 can (14 ounces) sweetened condensed milk

$^1/_3$ cup WATKINS Pure Cocoa

2 cups heavy whipping cream

1 cup half-and-half

1 tablespoon WATKINS Vanilla

Combine sweetened condensed milk and cocoa in medium saucepan. Cook over low heat, stirring constantly, for about 10 minutes or until mixture is smooth and slightly thickened. Remove from heat; cool slightly. Gradually add cream, half-and-half and vanilla, beating with whisk until well blended. Refrigerate until cold. Place in ice cream freezer container and freeze according to manufacturer's instructions.

Makes 1$^1/_2$ quarts (18 servings)

Watkins Cocoa Ice Cream

White Chocolate Mousse

1 cup vanilla milk chips *or* 7 ounces white chocolate, chopped

1/4 cup hot water

2 teaspoons WATKINS Vanilla

2 cups heavy whipping cream

1/2 cup sifted powdered sugar

Melt vanilla chips in top of double boiler or in microwave. Add hot water and vanilla; mix until smooth. Cool completely. Beat cream until it begins to thicken. Add sugar; continue beating until soft peaks form. Stir large spoonful of whipped cream into vanilla chip mixture, then fold mixture back into remaining whipped cream. Spoon mousse into individual custard cups or 4-cup mold. Refrigerate until thoroughly chilled. Serve cold.   *Makes 8 servings*

METRIC CONVERSION CHART

VOLUME MEASUREMENTS (dry)

1/8 teaspoon = 0.5 mL
1/4 teaspoon = 1 mL
1/2 teaspoon = 2 mL
3/4 teaspoon = 4 mL
1 teaspoon = 5 mL
1 tablespoon = 15 mL
2 tablespoons = 30 mL
1/4 cup = 60 mL
1/3 cup = 75 mL
1/2 cup = 125 mL
2/3 cup = 150 mL
3/4 cup = 175 mL
1 cup = 250 mL
2 cups = 1 pint = 500 mL
3 cups = 750 mL
4 cups = 1 quart = 1 L

VOLUME MEASUREMENTS (fluid)

1 fluid ounce (2 tablespoons) = 30 mL
4 fluid ounces (1/2 cup) = 125 mL
8 fluid ounces (1 cup) = 250 mL
12 fluid ounces (1 1/2 cups) = 375 mL
16 fluid ounces (2 cups) = 500 mL

WEIGHTS (mass)

1/2 ounce = 15 g
1 ounce = 30 g
3 ounces = 90 g
4 ounces = 120 g
8 ounces = 225 g
10 ounces = 285 g
12 ounces = 360 g
16 ounces = 1 pound = 450 g

DIMENSIONS

1/16 inch = 2 mm
1/8 inch = 3 mm
1/4 inch = 6 mm
1/2 inch = 1.5 cm
3/4 inch = 2 cm
1 inch = 2.5 cm

OVEN TEMPERATURES

250°F = 120°C
275°F = 140°C
300°F = 150°C
325°F = 160°C
350°F = 180°C
375°F = 190°C
400°F = 200°C
425°F = 220°C
450°F = 230°C

BAKING PAN SIZES

Utensil	Size in Inches/Quarts	Metric Volume	Size in Centimeters
Baking or	8×8×2	2 L	20×20×5
Cake Pan	9×9×2	2.5 L	23×23×5
(square or	12×8×2	3 L	30×20×5
rectangular)	13×9×2	3.5 L	33×23×5
Loaf Pan	8×4×3	1.5 L	20×10×7
	9×5×3	2 L	23×13×7
Round Layer	8×1½	1.2 L	20×4
Cake Pan	9×1½	1.5 L	23×4
Pie Plate	8×1¼	750 mL	20×3
	9×1¼	1 L	23×3
Baking Dish	1 quart	1 L	—
or Casserole	1½ quart	1.5 L	—
	2 quart	2 L	—